A CHILD'S INTRODUCTION TO

JAZZ

A CHILD'S INTRODUCTION TO

JAZZ

The Musicians, Culture, and Roots of
THE WORLD'S COOLEST MUSIC

Jabari Asim

Illustrated by Jerrard K. Polk

BLACK DOG
& LEVENTHAL
PUBLISHERS
NEW YORK

Black Dog & Leventhal Publishers
Hachette Book Group
1290 Avenue of the Americas
New York, NY 10104

www.hachettebookgroup.com
www.blackdogandleventhal.com

First Edition: December 2022

Black Dog & Leventhal Publishers is an imprint of Perseus Books, LLC, a subsidiary of Hachette Book Group, Inc.
The Black Dog & Leventhal Publishers name and logo are trademarks of Hachette Book Group, Inc.

The publisher is not responsible for websites (or their content) that are not owned by the publisher.

The Hachette Speakers Bureau provides a wide range of authors for speaking events.
To find out more, go to www.HachetteSpeakersBureau.com or call (866) 376-6591.

Print book interior design by Katie Benezra

Library of Congress Cataloging-in-Publication Data
Names: Asim, Jabari, 1962– author. | Polk, Jerrard K., illustrator.
Title: A child's introduction to jazz : the musicians, culture, and roots of the world's coolest music / Jabari Asim ; illustrated by Jerrard K. Polk.
Description: First edition. | New York, NY : Black Dog & Leventhal, 2022. | Includes index. | Audience: Ages 8–12 | Summary: "A Child's Introduction to Jazz explores the rich history of jazz music, including profiles of famous musicians like Louis Armstrong and Billie Holliday. Written by A Child's Introduction to African American History author Jabari Asim, the book includes downloadable links throughout, to allow kids to listen along to the instruments and musical flair of jazz"—Provided by publisher.
Identifiers: LCCN 2022012554 (print) | LCCN 2022012555 (ebook) | ISBN 9780762479412 (hardcover) | ISBN 9780762479429 (ebook)
Subjects: LCSH: Jazz—History and criticism—Juvenile literature. | Jazz musicians—Juvenile literature.
Classification: LCC ML3506 .A746 2022 (print) | LCC ML3506 (ebook) | DDC 781.65—dc23/eng/20220311
LC record available at https://lccn.loc.gov/2022012554
LC ebook record available at https://lccn.loc.gov/2022012555

ISBNs: 978-0-7624-7941-2 (hardcover); 978-0-7624-7942-9 (ebook)

Printed in China

APS

10 9 8 7 6 5 4 3 2 1

Jabari Asim's dedication

In memory of my brother Seitu,
who first taught me about
this wonderful music.

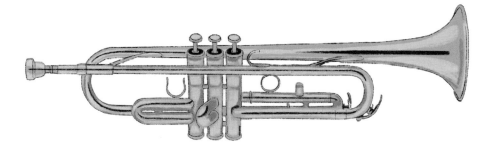

Jerrard K. Polk's dedication

To my wife, son, mom, and dad.
Thanks to JAZZ, a constant
source of inspiration!

LISTEN ALONG!

· ·

This interactive book allows you to listen to the sounds of jazz as you read! When you see the Listen Along boxes, ask your parent or guardian to scan the QR code to find a list of different jazz sounds. Click on the track to hear some cool instruments and sounds!

You can see the track list on our website: https://hach.co/ChildsIntroJazz

Contents

Introduction: Roots and Rhythm

Have you ever heard a woodpecker tapping on a tree trunk? The *tap-tap-tap* of its beak against the bark is what we call **rhythm**. Have you ever patted your foot while listening to a favorite tune? The pattern of sounds your foot makes is also what we call rhythm. The bark of a dog, the tick of a clock, and the *brisk-brisk* of a broom sweeping the sidewalk are all examples of the rhythms that can be heard throughout the day, indoors and out.

From Africa to New Orleans

No one can say for sure where or when people began to create rhythms of their own, perhaps by clapping their hands or pounding sticks together. We do know that rhythm has strong roots in Africa, home of the world's earliest civilizations. African rhythms traveled across the Atlantic when people were abducted from their homes and forced to sail to the Americas. One of the places they arrived was New Orleans, a port city on the Mississippi River, near the Gulf of Mexico. The Chitimacha people had lived there before being forced off the land by colonizers from France and Spain. New Orleans became part of the United States in 1803.

JAZZ PLAYLIST

There are so many cool jazz songs you can find and listen to. We'll talk about these musicians throughout the book.

"Maple Leaf Rag"
by Jelly Roll Morton

"West End Blues"
by Louis Armstrong

"Take The 'A' Train"
by Duke Ellington

"One O'Clock Jump"
by Count Basie

"Charleston"
by James P. Johnson

"Ain't Misbehavin'"
by Fats Waller

"A-Tisket, A-Tasket"
by Ella Fitzgerald

"Blue Moon"
by Billie Holiday

"Walkin' and Swingin'"
by Mary Lou Williams

"Salt Peanuts"
by Dizzy Gillespie
and Charlie Parker

"Misterioso"
by Thelonious Monk

"All Blues"
by Miles Davis

"Bag's Groove"
by Modern Jazz Quartet

"Take Five"
by Dave Brubeck

"Watermelon Man"
by Herbie Hancock

"My Favorite Things"
by John Coltrane

"Work Song"
by Cannonball Adderley

"Birdland"
by Weather Report

"Bells (Ring Loudly)"
by Terri Lyne Carrington

"If It's Magic"
by Cécile McLorin Salvant

Early Jazz

Jazz Beginnings

In some parts of the United States, Africans had been forbidden to play drums. Their captors worried that they would use rhythm to send messages to their enslaved kin and share plans to turn against the people who held them in bondage. New Orleans was one of the few places where drums were allowed to be played. Every Sunday, Black people would gather to make music and dance in that city's Congo Square. Some of the people were free and some of them were not. They brought rhythms they knew from various places in Africa. There, those rhythms came in contact with music from other places like Mexico, Cuba, and France, as well as the music of the Indigenous people who had lived in Louisiana for centuries. From this blend of sound, they developed the music often called "jazz." Some people prefer to call it "African American classical music," while others prefer "Great Black Music." No matter what it's called, this marvelous music took shape in New Orleans and, in time, its irresistible rhythms spread around the world.

Over the years, jazz musicians have experimented with different styles, favoring

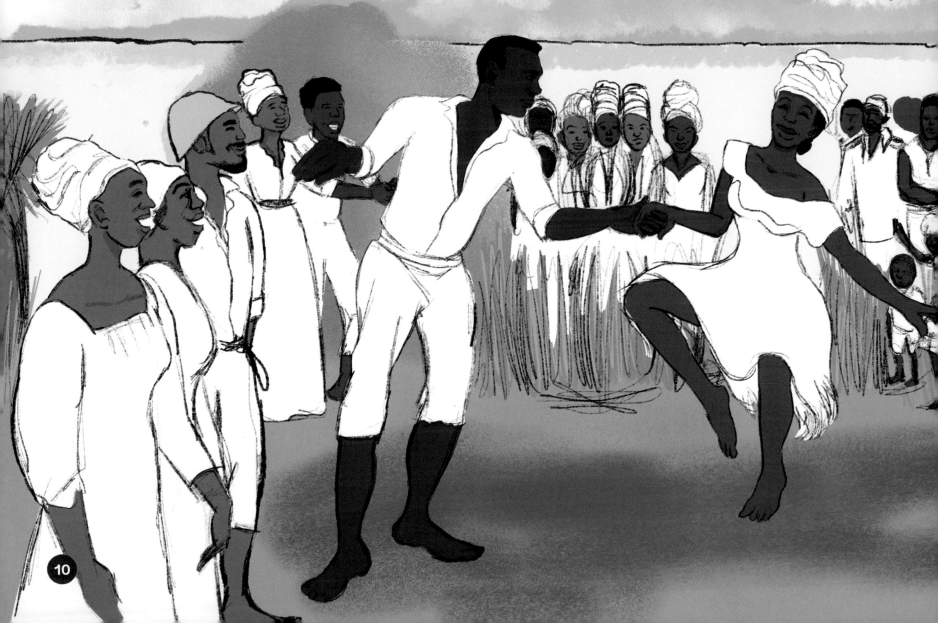

Early Instruments

some over others. They include Dixieland, swing, bebop, cool jazz, hard bop, free jazz, and fusion. In each style, the creators of this music were in search of a sound that pleased their ears and satisfied their imaginations. Duke Ellington, whom we will meet in these pages, perhaps said it best: "Music at its finest," he said, "is beyond category."

The musicians of Congo Square played instruments like those they, or their ancestors, had known in their homelands, as well as instruments first introduced in Europe. They included drums of various sizes, many of which were made of sheep or goat skin stretched over hollow logs;

gourds; animal jawbones; banjos; violins; and tambourines. There was also the reco-reco, an instrument made of wood or bamboo. Sounds were made by scraping notches along its sides with a stick. Some musicians even wore strings of bells wrapped around their legs.

LISTEN ALONG

Scan the QR code and click on track 1 to hear what the reco-reco sounds like.

Ragtime

Ragtime was a form of popular Black music that came before jazz. Interest in it began to decline around the time that jazz began to emerge. Its most prominent composer is **Scott Joplin**, who lived and worked in Missouri. He published "Maple Leaf Rag" in 1899. "The Entertainer" (1902) is his best-known song.

Another important figure was **James Reese Europe**. He directed Europe's Society Orchestra, a large ragtime band based in New York City. In 1912 they performed in Carnegie Hall, the city's most glamorous music venue. In 1913, the orchestra became one of the first African American bands to record its music. During World War I, James Reese Europe helped introduce France to Black music when he led the 369th Infantry Regiment band on a tour of that country. Both soldiers and musicians, they were also known as the Harlem Hellfighters.

▲ Scott Joplin

The First Jazz Musicians

Charles "Buddy" Bolden, also known as "King Bolden," is believed to be the first jazz musician. He first picked up a cornet in the 1890s, when he was in his teens. Soon he formed his own band and became a star performer whose concerts drew large crowds. At dance halls, parades, and fish fries, people danced and swayed as he played songs like "Didn't He Ramble" and "Buddy Bolden's Blues." His career did not last long, ending years before the first jazz recordings were made. Only one photograph of him is known to exist. He is shown with his band members, including a trombonist, a guitarist, two clarinetists, and an upright bass player.

Other talented cornetists soon followed, among them **Joe "King" Oliver**. Born in Louisiana in 1881, he grew up playing in New Orleans brass bands. As an adult, he started his own group, the Creole Jazz Band. In 1918, he took his act on the road to various cities before settling in Chicago.

Sidney Bechet was another gifted New Orleans musician who arrived in Chicago at nearly the same time as King Oliver. He started out as a cornetist before taking up the clarinet and the soprano sax. He helped spread the wonders of jazz not only across the country but also across the Atlantic to Europe. In 1919, he joined Will Marion Cook's Southern Syncopated Orchestra, performing for King George V in London. Bechet enjoyed a long career, eventually making his home in France.

THE GREAT MIGRATION

Many other African Americans were also heading north, leaving New Orleans and other places in the Southern state for cities like St. Louis, Chicago, and New York. Their journey, called **The Great Migration**, brought with it many habits and customs, including dance and music.

Louis Armstrong

Back in Chicago, King Oliver's band continued to attract fans. Their growing audience led to an exciting gig at Lincoln Gardens, a popular dance hall. In search of a bigger sound, Oliver decided to add another cornetist to the group. He wrote to a young musician in New Orleans and offered him a job. The young man's name was **Louis Armstrong**. The year was 1922. Soon jazz would never be the same.

Born into a poor family in 1901, young Louis was often on his own. In 1912, he was arrested and sent to the Colored Waif's Home for Boys. Already a gifted musician and singer, he learned to play the cornet during the eighteen months he spent there. Once free, Louis avoided hard labor by seeking jobs as a performer. He made a name for himself playing in some of the best-known bands in New Orleans and even on riverboats. When Oliver reached out to him from Chicago, he was ready.

After joining Oliver, Armstrong played in a recording studio for the first time in 1923. The young man soon upstaged the leader. He became known for his solos, playing with such skill that he stood out from the rest of the band. In time, he would become one of the most famous entertainers in the world.

Armstrong recorded his first songs as a bandleader in 1925. His solos on tunes like "Gut Bucket Blues" and "Muskrat Ramble" set the standard for generations of horn players to come.

Cornet or Trumpet?

In 1926, Armstrong switched permanently from one brass instrument, the cornet, to another, the trumpet. A cornet is smaller and rounder than a trumpet, which has a brighter, piercing sound. After Armstrong, most jazz musicians chose the trumpet over the cornet.

▲ Louis Armstrong and band musicians

▲ Cornet (top), trumpet (bottom)

LISTEN ALONG

Scan the QR code and click on track 2 to hear the trumpet.

The Hot Five

Armstrong's first recordings as a bandleader were made with a group known as the Hot Five. In addition to Armstrong, its members were Lil Hardin Armstrong on piano, Kid Ory on trombone, Johnny Dodds on clarinet, and Johnny St. Cyr on guitar and banjo. Lil was Armstrong's wife and wrote some of the band's most popular songs, such as "Struttin' with Some Barbecue" and "Just for a Thrill."

Role Model

After the success of his Hot Five recordings, Armstrong continued to work in the studio with other talented bandmates, including the pianist **Earl "Fatha" Hines**. On songs like "West End Blues" and "Weather Bird," he perfected his powerful trumpet technique, which would influence jazz musicians for decades—and not just trumpeters. The same is true of his singing style, which had a huge impact on the jazz singers who came along after him.

His long career included co-starring roles in movies and Broadway plays, as well as showstopping performances before music lovers around the world. Louis Armstrong is still revered as one of the greatest ever, a giant of American music.

JELLY ROLL MORTON

Another pioneer of jazz was Ferdinand Joseph LaMothe, better known as Jelly Roll Morton. Born in New Orleans around 1890, Morton was a brilliant composer and pianist. He was a colorful character who dressed in flashy clothes and sported a diamond in his tooth. With his band the Red Hot Peppers and with other groups, Morton traveled often and recorded more than one hundred of his compositions. His songs, including "King Porter Stomp" and "Sidewalk Blues," are still played by modern jazz musicians.

Second Lines

As far back as the 1800s, African Americans in New Orleans formed social clubs and "benevolent societies" to take care of their members' needs. When a member passed away, the societies often conducted funeral parades, which had roots in African culture. Brass bands and drummers processed through the streets, accompanying the deceased to the burial ground. A second line of people followed the drums and horns, dancing and gesturing with handkerchiefs and parasols. Early jazz musicians sometimes played in these "Second Line" parades and borrowed rhythms to use in their own performances. The events are still a part of New Orleans culture to this day.

LISTEN ALONG

Scan the QR code and click on track 3 to hear what a New Orleans marching band sounds like.

Jazz on Broadway

Jazz musicians quickly made their presence known on Broadway, the main theater district in New York City. Noble Sissle and Eubie Blake composed the music and lyrics for *Shuffle Along*, the first all-Black hit show. The production, which premiered in 1921, included several major stars of the era, including Paul Robeson, Adelaide Hall, and Josephine Baker. Another jazz musician, Will Marion Cook, had also composed for Broadway productions, including *In Dahomey*, but none as popular as *Shuffle Along*, which ran for 504 performances.

▶ *Shuffle Along*

Race Records

The success of blues recordings helped make it possible for jazz performers to make records too. In the early 1920s, three Black singers were among the most popular entertainers in the country.

The first of them was **Mamie Smith**. Her song "Crazy Blues" sold more than one million copies.

The second was **Gertrude "Ma" Rainey**. Traveling with her own tent, she put on splashy shows with dancing girls and glittery costumes that dazzled the crowds. She made almost one hundred recordings, sometimes working with Louis Armstrong and other jazz musicians. "See See Rider Blues" was one of her best-loved songs.

The third was **Bessie Smith**, often considered the greatest classic blues singer ever. Ma Rainey helped her get started in show business and gave her advice about how to perform. Smith also recorded with Louis Armstrong. Her hits included "Downhearted Blues" and "Reckless Blues."

These women's songs became known as "race records." Their popularity proved that Black music also appealed to audiences of all kinds.

▲ Gertrude "Ma" Rainey (center)

"Father of the Blues"

Another of Bessie Smith's hits was "St. Louis Blues," composed by **W.C. Handy**. A cornetist and songwriter, he was so inspired by the record's success that he helped produce a short film by the same name, starring Smith. It played in movie houses from 1929 to 1932. Handy called himself "The Father of the Blues," and while he was not a jazz composer, many of his songs were adopted by jazz musicians. He was also one of the first Black musicians to publish and profit from his own creations. Other historic Handy compositions include "Beale Street Blues" and "Yellow Dog Blues."

IMPROVISATION

When improvising, musicians invent new melodies on the spot. They often do this when performing a solo while the **rhythm section** (usually drums, bass, and piano or guitar) maintains the beat. Improvisations take place in many forms of music, but they are seldom as complex as those heard in jazz. We will meet many great jazz improvisers in these pages, including Charlie Parker, John Coltrane, and Miles Davis.

LISTEN ALONG

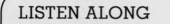

Scan the QR code and click on track 4 to hear what a rhythm section sounds like.

Harlem and the Beginnings of Big Band

Harlem Happenings

While Americans went wild for race records, Black people continued to head north by the thousands. Many of them settled in in Harlem, a neighborhood in New York City. It soon became the capital of Black America.

▲ James P. Johnson, Art Tatum, Willie "The Lion" Smith, and Thomas "Fats" Waller

Rent Parties and Cutting Contests

Musicians joined workers of all kinds in Harlem's crowded tenement buildings, looking for a chance to make a living. They played an important role as entertainers during "rent parties," organized by lodgers to help pay their monthly bills. Partygoers paid a small fee (usually a few coins) for the opportunity to drink, mingle, and dance to live music. Often it was provided by a pianist who played in a style called "stride." To master the rollicking, fast-paced music, a pianist had to have nimble fingers and an entertaining personality. **Willie "The Lion" Smith** and **James P. Johnson** were two of the best.

Smith was a champion of "cutting contests," competitions in which pianists tried to outplay each other in front of a boisterous crowd. "The Lion" strutted to the keyboard with confidence, a cigar clenched between his teeth. More often than not, he was crowned the winner at the end of the evening.

Johnson was a gifted songwriter. His compositions included "Carolina Shout," "Charleston," and other songs that were popular during the 1920s and 1930s. He was also a teacher. One of his best pupils was **Thomas "Fats" Waller**. A talented organist and composer as well as a pianist, Waller was also a funny, outgoing performer. He began to write songs while he was still a teenager. By the end of his more than twenty-year career, he had created many popular hits that are still performed today, including "Ain't Misbehavin'" and "Honeysuckle Rose."

A legendary cutting contest took place in 1932, when Johnson, Waller, and "The Lion" gathered at Morgan's bar. They met there to test the skills of **Art Tatum**, 23 years old and newly arrived from Ohio. To the amazement of everyone, Tatum outplayed the famous trio. It was the beginning of a busy, productive career. Tatum recorded hundreds of songs that showed off his great speed and knack for harmonies. By the time of his death at age 47, he had created a body of work that secured his place among the greatest jazz pianists of all time.

Swing Was the Thing

The 1920s also marked the beginning of the Jazz Age, when fun-seekers flocked to ballrooms to dance to the music of **big bands**. The bands were led by some of the most talented artists of the era. From the mid-1930s to the end of the 1940s, the dominant style of jazz, highly rhythmic and easy to dance to, came to be known as **swing**. When asked what swing meant, Louis Armstrong replied, "If you don't feel it, you'll never know it."

LISTEN ALONG

Scan the QR code and click on track 5 to hear a swinging jazz orchestra.

On the Bandstand

Big bands usually contained at least ten pieces. The largest usually contained five saxophones, four trumpets, four trombones, and four rhythm instruments (piano, bass, drums, guitar)—some seventeen instruments in all. Three kinds of saxophones were featured, including two altos, two tenors, and one baritone.

Alto
Saxophones

Tenor
Saxophones

Baritone
Saxophone

Guitar

Bass

Trumpets

Trombones

Piano

Drums

A Band Is Born

The **Fletcher Henderson Orchestra** was one of the earliest and best of these bands. It played at the Club Alabam in New York City before moving on to the Roseland Ballroom. Louis Armstrong joined the group for a time. So did **Coleman Hawkins**, who became known as the king of the saxophone. He played with Henderson for about ten years.

The Inventor

In 1846, **Antoine-Joseph Sax** filed a patent in France for the saxophone, one of many instruments he invented. He never made much money from his devices, but the sax, as it came to be called, grew in popularity.

It could be found in many bands by the turn of the twentieth century. Unlike the trumpet, it was seldom featured as a solo instrument. That changed when Coleman Hawkins developed a technique that set the standard for decades to come. Like Sidney Bechet and **Johnny Hodges**, Hawkins was recognized as one of the very best at his instrument. His best-known song is "Body and Soul."

▸ Antoine-Joseph Sax

Early Sax Superstars

Soprano sax: Sidney Bechet

Alto sax: Johnny Hodges

Tenor sax: Coleman Hawkins

The Savoy Ballroom

At the Savoy Ballroom in Harlem, **Chick Webb**'s band was the main attraction. As a boy in Baltimore, William Henry "Chick" Webb had taken up drumming to strengthen his badly injured back. His talent soon took him to New York. For four years his band had been drawing crowds, including dancers who showed off their moves on the Savoy's huge dance floor. Then he hired a teenage singer named **Ella Fitzgerald**. He paid her twelve dollars and fifty cents a week.

The First Lady of Song

The young lady with the sweet, clear voice soon became the star of the show. In 1938 her first hit, "A-Tisket, A-Tasket," sold more than one million copies and stayed at the number one spot on the charts for seventeen weeks. Ella was just 21 years old. When Webb died in 1939, Ella led the band for another three years.

She went on to enjoy a long and fruitful career as one of the most celebrated singers in the world. She worked with many of the best musicians of her time, including Louis Armstrong, Dizzy Gillespie, Count Basie, and many others. A series of albums dedicated to the work of Cole Porter, George and Ira Gershwin, and other great songwriters

were among her most popular recordings. She toured and performed until 1991, when illness forced her to retire. She recorded more than 200 albums in all.

▼ Ella Fitzgerald

Ella and Marilyn

During the 1940s and 1950s, Ella was one of the most popular singers in the world. Despite her fame, some nightclub owners wouldn't allow her to perform in their spaces. One such club in Los Angeles was called the Mocambo. Its owner refused to hire her until he received a call from Marilyn Monroe, a world-famous movie star. She promised to sit in the front row every night if Ella was invited to sing. The owner agreed, and Marilyn kept her promise. Her presence in the front row brought valuable attention to the Mocambo and new opportunities for Ella. Afterward, she never had to perform in a small jazz club again.

Scat Singing

Audiences loved it when Ella sang without words, and chose instead to imitate the sound of a horn. This technique, often performed by jazz vocalists, is called **scat singing**. Although Louis Armstrong wasn't the first scat singer, he is credited with making it popular. An early example is his scatting on "Heebie Jeebies," a song he recorded in 1926. Ten years later, Ella tried it on a recording of "(If You Can't Sing It) You'll Have to Swing It." Cab Calloway and Sarah Vaughn, among others, were also acclaimed for their scat singing.

LISTEN ALONG

Scan the QR code and click on track 6 to hear scat singing.

LINDY HOPPERS

At the Savoy and other ballrooms, dancers rocked and spun with such abandon that they wore grooves into the dance floor. The Lindy Hop was the most popular style of dance in the 1930s and 1940s. Each hopper had their own individual style, but most moves involved fast footwork, hand-to-hand dancing, flips, and splits, all to the beat of the band. Some of the best-known Lindy Hoppers included Leon James, Ann Johnson, and Norma Miller. The song "Stompin' at the Savoy" celebrates this era. Composed by Edgar Sampson, it was first recorded by Chick Webb in 1934.

▲ Duke Ellington at the Cotton Club

Duke Ellington

At the Savoy, huge crowds gathered on nights when Chick Webb's orchestra competed against others in a battle of the bands. On March 7, 1937, Webb suffered a rare defeat, losing to the Duke Ellington Orchestra. By then, Ellington had gotten used to leading his group to victory.

Born in Washington, D.C., in 1899, Edward Kennedy Ellington worked as a sign-painter before establishing himself as a pianist and bandleader in his hometown. He sought his fortune in New York City, landing a job playing piano for blues singer Ada Louise Smith. By 1924, he had a regular job at Club Kentucky, leading his own six-piece band. He got a big break at the end of 1927, when his orchestra became the house band at the Cotton Club. Perhaps the fanciest club in Harlem, its owners hired Black entertainers but didn't allow Black customers. To meet the club's requirements, Ellington expanded his band to eleven players. Weekly radio broadcasts from the Cotton Club helped make him the best-known Black musician in the country.

Because he was a highly respected composer and leader, Ellington had no trouble attracting first-rate talent. Many of his musicians remained with the band for years. Early standouts included **James "Bubber" Miley** (trumpet), **Joe "Tricky Sam" Nanton** (trombone), and Johnny Hodges (alto sax).

LISTEN ALONG

Scan the QR code and click on track 7 to hear the jazz piano.

Meet Bricktop

The full name of Ellington's first employer was Ada Beatrice Queen Victoria Louise Virginia Smith. She was better known as "Bricktop," so nicknamed for her bright red hair and freckles. A dancer as well as a singer, she started performing professionally at age 16 and continued into her 80s. Her peak years were in Paris, where she moved soon after meeting Ellington. She owned and operated a series of popular nightclubs featuring jazz and other live entertainment. Her most notable club, Chez Bricktop, regularly drew large crowds. As one of the most popular African Americans in Europe, her friends and patrons included Langston Hughes, Cole Porter, and Josephine Baker.

▲ Bricktop

American Standards

A **standard** is a composition so well-known that it's considered a permanent part of a musical tradition. No songwriter has composed as many jazz standards as Duke Ellington. These are just a few of those he composed during the early years of his stardom. Many more were to come.

"East St. Louis Toodle-Oo" (1926)

"Mood Indigo" (1930)

"It Don't Mean a Thing (If It Ain't Got That Swing)" (1931)

Globe-Trotters

Duke Ellington's orchestra performed six nights a week at the Cotton Club, staying until 1931. That year he took his band on a cross-country tour, playing up to five shows in a single day. In 1933 they spent forty-six days in Europe, where they thrilled large crowds. They returned to that continent for a month in 1939, playing in France, Belgium, the Netherlands, Sweden, Denmark, and Norway.

The late 1930s and 1940s were very productive for Ellington. During that time, his orchestra included a number of impressive musicians. Three of the best were **Charles "Cootie" Williams** (trumpet), **Jimmy Blanton** (bass), and **Ben Webster** (tenor sax).

Ellington began one of the most important partnerships of his career when **Billy Strayhorn** arrived in 1938. Strayhorn stayed on for nearly thirty years, working as an arranger, lyricist, and pianist. One of the most gifted composers of his time, he wrote several standards, including "A Flower is a Lovesome Thing," "Chelsea Bridge," and "Take the 'A' Train," which became the orchestra's signature tune.

▶ Billy Strayhorn and Duke Ellington

▲ Cab Calloway with his orchestra

The Cab Calloway Orchestra

The Cab Calloway Orchestra became the house band at the Cotton Club when Ellington and his players left in 1931. A high-energy performer with a dazzling smile, Calloway often appeared onstage in white tie and tails. In his time, he was famous for "Minnie the Moocher," in which he sings the phrase "hi-de-hi-de-ho." Not just a talented singer, he was also a skillful bandleader. His orchestra included some of the best instrumentalists in the business, including Dizzy Gillespie and bassist **Milt Hinton**. He appeared in several movies, including *St. Louis Blues* and the classic *Stormy Weather*. In 1948, he disbanded his orchestra in favor of a small combo. He also performed starring roles in several plays, including *Porgy and Bess* and *Hello, Dolly!*. His best-known songs include "Blues in the Night" and "Jumpin' Jive."

WHAT DO ARRANGERS DO?

Arrangers shape a piece of music to fit a performer's needs. This may involve several activities, including altering the tempo and rhythm of a song, or reworking it to highlight certain instruments. Arrangers must be familiar with a band's strengths and weaknesses, as well as the bandleader's preferences.

There have been many gifted jazz arrangers, including **Fletcher Henderson**, **Billy Strayhorn**, and **Gil Evans**.

American Genius

When the public's love for big bands faded, Ellington continued to thrive. He composed and recorded until the end of his life, earning much acclaim along the way. He became an ambassador of jazz, sharing the beautiful music with willing listeners around the world. More than once, heads of state awarded him their nation's highest honors. By the time of his death in 1974, he had written or co-written more than 1,000 songs. No discussion of America's greatest composers would be complete without mention—and praise—of Duke Ellington.

Bix Beiderbecke

Like the Ellington orchestra, most big bands had stars who could be relied on to unleash show-stopping solos. For **Paul Whiteman and His Orchestra**, that star was Bix Beiderbecke. Born in Davenport, Iowa, in 1903, Leon Bismark Beiderbecke taught himself to play cornet and piano. He reached a turning point at age 17, when he saw Louis Armstrong playing cornet with a riverboat band. He earned considerable attention playing with the Wolverine Orchestra in the Midwest and in New York before joining forces with Whiteman. He was featured in Whiteman's band from 1927 to 1930. His best-known songs include "Singin' the Blues" and "In a Mist."

▲ Duke Ellington visited musicians in Pakistan when he was an ambassador of jazz.

WHAT DO LYRICISTS DO?

Duke Ellington and many other jazz composers seldom wrote words for the songs they composed. They left that role to lyricists, who are as skillful with words as composers are with musical notes. Billy Strayhorn was that rare composer who also wrote excellent lyrics. Classic examples of his work include "My Little Brown Book," "Something to Live For," and "Lush Life," probably his best-known ballad.

Another brilliant lyricist was **Andy Razaf**, who frequently partnered with Fats Waller, Eubie Blake, and other jazz composers. Razaf sold his first song when he was still a teenager and working as an elevator operator. His songs include "Ain't Misbehavin'," "This Joint Is Jumpin'," and "(What Did I Do to Be So) Black and Blue," believed to be one of the first songs to protest the unfair treatment of African Americans.

JAZZ ACROSS THE ATLANTIC

Meanwhile, Europeans had begun to develop their own jazz scene, with their own talent. The most prominent group, the Quintette du Hot Club de France, had two breakout stars, guitarist **Django Reinhardt** and **Stéphane Grappelli**, a violinist. Grappelli took up his instrument at age 12. After three years of formal study, he began busking, or performing on the streets to earn money from passers-by. He found work playing along to silent movies, then was introduced to jazz when he heard a record playing in a restaurant.

Jean "Django" Reinhardt, born in Belgium in 1910, learned guitar by watching seasoned players in his community and copying their movements. Like Grappelli, he became a busker at age 15, playing for coins in local cafes. Reinhardt first heard jazz around 1930, when he listened to a friend's records featuring Ellington, Armstrong, and other masters of the music. Fascinated, he began to practice what he'd heard.

Grappelli and Reinhardt joined forces in London in 1934. They made several successful albums with the Quintette, as well as with American stars like Coleman Hawkins. Their band lasted until 1939, when World War II broke out in Europe. Although the duo played together again after the war, the original Quintette never re-formed. The two men last recorded together in 1949. Reinhardt died in 1953 and is still praised for his unique style. Grappelli went on to have a remarkably long career, touring and recording for sixty years.

◄ Stéphane Grappelli and Django Reinhardt

Kansas City Jazz

Meanwhile, musicians in the Midwest were developing a scene of their own, especially in Kansas City, Missouri. That town had become nearly as important as Chicago and New York in the growth of jazz. Some of the key players made their way to New York and took the city by storm.

He was born in New Jersey, but **William "Count" Basie** came of age in the Midwest and South during the late 1920s. Basie found work there in a band called the Blue Devils, before switching to another band based in Kansas City led by Bennie Moten. When Moten died in 1935, many of his musicians began to work together under Basie's leadership. The following year, he took the group to Chicago, expanding it from nine to thirteen players. In 1937 they headlined in New York at the Roseland Ballroom and recorded several tunes that made them enormously popular. For the next several decades they were among the most revered jazz bands in existence, perhaps second only to the Duke Ellington Orchestra. In 1961 the Count Basie Orchestra performed at an inauguration ball for President John F. Kennedy. Basie continued to lead the band until 1983. "One O'Clock Jump," "Jumpin' at the Woodside," and "Every Day I Have the Blues" are among his most notable songs.

Mary Lou Williams was one of the few women instrumentalists working in jazz. Born in Pittsburgh, she came to Kansas City in the late 1920s with her husband, a saxophonist. She was offered work as an arranger and backup pianist for Andy Kirk and His Clouds of Joy. She stayed with the group for more than a decade before making her way to New York.

She became an in-demand arranger, working for Louis Armstrong and Benny Goodman, among others. She wrote arrangements for as many as six bands a week while traveling on the road as a working pianist. As the band covered as many as 500 miles in a single night, she wrote in the car by flashlight. Eventually she also worked for

▲ **William "Count" Basie and Mary Lou Williams**

Duke Ellington, arranging forty-seven songs for him. These days she might be as well known for her composing and arranging as for her playing. Her compositions include "Zodiac Suite," "Froggy Bottom," and "Music for Peace" (also known as "Mary Lou's Mass").

Lester Young is perhaps the most notable artist to emerge from the Kansas City jazz community. Born in Mississippi and raised in New Orleans, Young had to help support his family from age 5. He had been working odd jobs for several years when he joined his father's circus band at age 10. He taught himself a number of instruments but focused on the tenor sax in his late teens. Like Count Basie, he played in the Blue Devils. His big break came when he replaced Coleman Hawkins in Fletcher Henderson's band. But his sensitive, thoughtful way of playing didn't fit the group's style. He didn't become a star until he rejoined Basie's band. He also played in small-group sessions with pianist/singer Nat "King" Cole, guitarist Charlie Christian, and others. Today he is best remembered for his partnership with Billie Holiday. They were close friends who gave each other famous nicknames. Holiday called him "Prez." He called her "Lady Day."

INTERNATIONAL SWEETHEARTS OF RHYTHM

. . . .

This all-woman brass band was founded in 1938 to raise funds for a school for poor and Black children in Piney Woods, Mississippi. The first members were mostly Black or Asian. They included Helen Jones, Millie Jones, Willie Mae Wong, and star trumpeter Ernestine Carroll, also known as Tiny Davis. In 1943, they added white musicians as well, including saxophonist Rosalind Cron. The original lineup toured until 1949, playing before admiring crowds in Europe, New York, and Chicago. Audiences were sometimes less friendly in the American South. Few recordings of the band exist.

31

Strange Fruit

Born Eleanora Fagan in Philadelphia, **Billie Holiday** was celebrated for her elegant, emotional sound. She sang with deep feeling and careful attention to the meaning of a song's lyrics. She performed with many of the best jazz musicians over the course of her career, including Count Basie, Coleman Hawkins, and Ben Webster. Her recordings with Lester Young, however, are always counted among her best. They include "All of Me," "This Year's Kisses," and "Getting Some Fun Out of Life." Still, her song remembered above all others is probably "Strange Fruit." By the time she recorded it in 1939, more than 4,000 Black people had been killed by white mobs, a form of murder called lynching. The song, sung hauntingly by Holiday, takes painful note of these killings. Others have sung "Strange Fruit," but no one has performed it like Holiday did.

▶ **Billie Holiday and Lester Young**

Roy Eldridge

Billie Holiday's career had received a boost when she toured with Artie Shaw, a popular white bandleader willing to hire Black musicians. Six years after Holiday's stint with Shaw, Roy Eldridge came aboard. In 1944, jazz was still as segregated as America was. In most instances, white musicians played in white bands while Black musicians played in Black ones. Eldridge's work with Shaw and Gene Krupa, another white bandleader, helped push back against racial separation. He also excelled in small-group settings with other standouts, including Johnny Hodges and Art Tatum. For many listeners, Eldridge was the most gifted trumpeter since Louis Armstrong. His most acclaimed songs include "Wabash Stomp" and "Heckler's Hop."

◀ **Roy Eldridge, Gene Krupa, and Artie Shaw**

SPIRITUALS TO SWING

On December 23, 1938, music producer John Hammond organized *From Spirituals to Swing*, a historic concert presented to an integrated audience in New York's Carnegie Hall. The event was intended to showcase African Americans' contribution to their nation's musical culture. Hammond included performers of various kinds of Black music. For example, Count Basie and Oran "Hot Lips" Page played jazz, Big Bill Broonzy played the blues, and Sister Rosetta Tharpe sang gospel songs. Other performers were on hand as well. The concert was a smashing success, and Hammond presented it again the following year.

▲ Carnegie Hall in 1938
▶ Big Bill Broonzy

The Benny Goodman Orchestra

The Benny Goodman Orchestra enjoyed opportunities that no Black band could. By 1936 it was the most popular band in America. A gifted clarinetist as well as a bandleader, **Benny Goodman** worked to include African American musical styles by purchasing some of Fletcher Henderson's arrangements and hiring him to write more. Like Artie Shaw, he also hired Black musicians to join him on the bandstand. They included pianist Teddy Wilson, hired into Goodman's trio in 1936, **Lionel Hampton**, who integrated Goodman's quartet in 1938, and guitarist Charlie Christian, who joined Goodman's sextet in 1939.

▲ Benny Goodman with his orchestra

GOOD VIBES

Originally a drummer, Lionel Hampton became the first of the great vibraphonists.

Sometimes called "vibes," a **vibraphone** is a percussion instrument made of tuned metal bars. Sound is produced by striking them with soft mallets. It is played more often in jazz than perhaps any other form of music. Here are four of the best vibraphonists and examples of their work.

Lionel Hampton, "Flying Home"

Milt Jackson, "Bag's Groove"

Gary Burton, "Crystal Silence"

Stefon Harris, "Black Action Figure"

Charlie Christian is widely considered one of the most important electric guitarists of all time. However, he had a very short career. He was able to record only a few songs, most of them with Benny Goodman. He had just begun to experiment with new techniques when he died of tuberculosis in 1941 at age 25. His notable songs include "Stompin' at the Savoy" and "Solo Flight."

◄ Charlie Christian

The Bebop Era

LISTEN ALONG

Scan the QR code and click on track 8 to hear an example of bebop.

As the 1950s approached, big-band jazz would become less popular, giving way to rock and roll and pop music. As we shall see, some big bands continued to perform for decades, and some new ones emerged as well. Jazz itself was also beginning to change, as young performers searched for new ways to express themselves.

In the middle of these changing times, **Earl "Fatha" Hines** briefly enjoyed success with his big band. A veteran pianist who had recorded with Louis Armstrong, Hines welcomed new talent and new sounds. In 1942 he hired several newcomers who would become big names in jazz.

The Divine One

Hines's new vocalist was also a gifted backup pianist for the band. Just a teenager, **Sarah Vaughan** caught his attention when she won an amateur singing contest at Harlem's legendary Apollo Theater. Her powerful voice covered a wide range of notes, and she was a skillful scat singer, able to match the speed and timbre of the horns in the band. She quickly established herself as one of the most gifted singers of her generation. Her notable songs include "Broken Hearted Melody" and "Send in the Clowns."

Vaughan then joined forces with **Billy Eckstine**, who had also been in the Hines band. She left Eckstine's band in 1944 to begin a long solo career. Eckstine was a charming entertainer with a rich, baritone voice. His best-known songs include "Jelly, Jelly" and "I Apologize." When Eckstine left Hines to form his own orchestra, he brought a young horn player with him.

▲ Sarah Vaughan

Dizzy Gillespie

That horn player became the most important trumpeter since Roy Eldridge. John Birks Gillespie, better known as Dizzy, was born in South Carolina in 1917. He started playing trumpet at age 12, moved to New York at 19, and by his early twenties had proved himself enough to win a place in various professional big bands. In addition to playing with Earl Hines, he played in the Cab Calloway and Billy Eckstine orchestras. With his trademark beret, horn-rimmed glasses, and fondness for jokes, Dizzy quickly became an easily recognized jazz star.

He was playing in Cab Calloway's band when he met Charlie "Bird" Parker. Soon after, they teamed up on the Hines bandstand. Sharing a desire to push jazz in a new direction, they became close friends and musical partners. Starting in 1944, they worked on the new sound, mostly in small groups of four or five. Some of the older musicians didn't approve of what they were doing, but the young artists pushed on. They recorded new work in studios, played in clubs in New York and Los Angeles, and practiced in the late evening after most venues had closed.

◀ Dizzy Gillespie

TRUMPETS

Dizzy Gillespie cast a huge shadow over other trumpeters during this period. Still, others emerged to display their sparkling talents. They include Clifford Brown, Fats Navarro, and Joe Guy.

Charlie Parker

Growing up in Kansas City, Missouri, in the 1920s and 1930s, Parker didn't take to the alto saxophone at first. He liked the instrument but struggled to keep up with the serious players in his community. Some of them grew impatient with his efforts and even made fun of him. Ashamed but determined, he practiced and practiced until he, at last, was ready. By 1940, he had developed a style that was all his own.

Harlem Jam Sessions

Parker and Dizzy Gillespie held jam sessions in Minton's Playhouse and Monroe's Uptown House, two nightclubs in Harlem. Away from crowds and the bright lights of the stage, they were free to try out new ideas. The music was fast-paced and difficult. Players who couldn't keep up were quickly cast aside. In time, a circle of musicians with similar ideas began to form. Let's meet some of them.

◄ **Charlie Parker**

Thelonious Monk, the house pianist at Minton's, was 23 years old. Although he was an active participant in the jam sessions, Monk's best years came later, in the 1950s and 1960s. He had an unusual style that audiences took a while to appreciate. In 1957 he performed a legendary engagement with his quartet at the Five Spot Café in New York City. For six months, huge crowds lined the sidewalks before packing the room to see the band play. By 1964, Monk was so famous that he was featured on the cover of *Time* magazine. His impressive playing aside, he is greatly respected as a composer. Many of the songs he wrote or co-wrote are now standards, including "Epistrophy," "Straight, No Chaser," and "Round Midnight."

► **Thelonious Monk**

Earl "Bud" Powell, born in New York City in 1924, was still in his teens when he found his way to Minton's. At first, he was not welcome among the more seasoned players, but Monk embraced the young pianist and encouraged the others to do the same. In due time, his style became closely linked to the new sound. Long after the end of his career, up-and-coming pianists would work hard to absorb his best methods. He played with such energy and speed that it could almost look as if he were attacking the piano. His many classic recordings include "Un Poco Loco," "Tempus Fugue-It," and "Dance of the Infidels."

Charlie Christian, whom we met earlier as a star of Benny Goodman's sextet, also played an important role. One of the last examples of his genius took place at Minton's in May 1941, when his version of "Stompin' at the Savoy" was recorded. It is treasured as classic by jazz fans.

A key player on Christian's last recording was **Kenny Clarke**, the house drummer at Minton's. During the after-hours jam sessions, he introduced new techniques that changed jazz—and jazz drumming—forever. He had a propulsive style that mixed a light, steady touch on the cymbals with explosive bursts of percussion that the other players called "bombs." Before Clarke, drummers relied on the bass drum or high-hat cymbal to keep time. After him, they copied his method of using the ride cymbal instead. Clarke was drafted into military service in 1943. He returned to the jazz scene in New York afterward, but eventually settled in France where he led a band for decades.

Max Roach became the house drummer at Monroe's Uptown House when he was still a teenager. Aside from Kenny Clarke, he was the drummer most often at the center of Dizzy and Bird's jam sessions. Born in North Carolina in 1924 and raised in Brooklyn, New York, his music lessons began at age 8 with piano lessons in a neighborhood church. He had switched to drums by age 10. His long career included many firsts. He became one of the first jazz musicians to become a college professor when he joined the faculty of University of Massachusetts at Amherst in 1972. In 1988, he became the first jazz musician to receive a fellowship from the MacArthur Foundation. One highlight of his sterling career is his album, *We Insist! Max Roach's Freedom Now Suite*. It combines first-rate music with strong lyrics and poetry about politics and history. Some people spoke out against the project, but Roach confidently defended it. "We American jazz musicians of African descent have proved beyond all doubt that we're master musicians of our instruments," he said. "Now what we have to do is employ our skill to tell the dramatic story of our people and what we've been through."

Bebop Instruments

Drum Kit

A jazz drummer's kit typically includes a small bass drum, two toms, a snare, two ride cymbals, and a high-hat. These are struck with sticks, brushes, or mallets.

Blowing the Saxophone

As time passed and the new sound spread from jam sessions to recordings and public performances, more musicians emerged to spread the new sound. Among the saxophonists, Sonny Stitt, Frank Morgan, and Jimmy Heath are names to know.

A tenor saxophonist, **Dexter Gordon** played with Louis Armstrong, Fletcher Henderson, and Lionel Hampton's big bands before he even got to New York in 1944. Once there, he played with Billy Eckstine's orchestra before jamming at Minton's and recording with Dizzy Gillespie. He didn't play much during the 1950s, but returned in the 1960s and played with success for many years in Europe. He came back to the United States in 1976 to great applause. He played before large crowds until illness slowed him down in the 1980s. Surprisingly, he began an acting career, appearing on the big screen in 'Round Midnight. His performance in the story of a troubled musician earned him an Academy Award nomination for Best Actor in a Leading Role in 1987.

The Tricky Trombone

The pace of the new music made it difficult to play on trombone. Only the most skilled could move the slide fast enough to keep up with the fast changes in tempo and rhythm. Bennie Green, J.J. Johnson, and Kai Winding were three of the best.

Up to this point, most of the women instrumentalists in jazz played the piano. An exception was trombonist **Melba Liston**.

She fell in love with the instrument as a young girl growing up in Kansas City, Missouri. She started taking lessons in school at age 7, and by 16 was performing professionally in California. During the 1940s, 1950s, and 1960s she toured with Dizzy Gillespie, Count Basie, and Billie Holiday, among others. For a short time she led an all-woman quintet. Although she was widely respected as a trombonist, she

▲ Melba Liston

was also in demand as a composer and arranger. She focused on
both roles for many years, spending less time playing trombone. She
wrote and arranged for jazz bandleaders such as Randy Weston and
Quincy Jones, while also working with pop singers like Diana Ross
and Marvin Gaye. She made music until the 1980s, when illness
forced her to retire. Her notable songs include "Blues Melba" and
"You Don't Say."

The Double Bass

The **bass**, often called the double bass, is the largest and lowest-
pitched instrument of the violin family. Although the bow is used in
jazz, in most instances the strings are plucked, a technique called
pizzicato. The shift away from swing music created opportunities
for bass players with power and range. That group included Oscar
Pettiford, Ray Brown, and Red Callender.

▲ Oscar Pettiford

When pop tunes took over the radio stations and seized the attention of music fans, Nat King Cole smoothly made the switch as well. As leader of the King Cole Trio in the 1940s and 1950s, he was a highly respected pianist. In 1946 he starred on *King Cole Trio Time* on NBC radio, something no Black musician had ever done before. He was also an excellent singer with a silky voice and a charming, elegant personality. He became one of the first African Americans to star in a television program when he hosted a variety show in 1956. It ended the following year because advertisers were reluctant to sponsor a show featuring a Black entertainer. Cole didn't let the rejection slow him down. He went on to appear in six movies, even playing W.C. Handy in the 1958 film *St. Louis Blues.* He also continued to sing and play before large audiences around the world. By the time of his death in 1965, he had sold more than 50 million records. His hit songs include: "Mona Lisa," "(Get Your Kicks on) Route 66," and "Straighten Up and Fly Right."

The Legacy of Dizzy and Bird

The ways that Charlie "Bird" Parker changed saxophone playing can be heard in the sound of nearly every important horn player to come along since. His life, however, was short in comparison. He died in 1955, at age 34. Dizzy Gillespie lived and played for decades more. In time he became an elder statesman for jazz, introducing it to new audiences in his travels around the world. Celebrated for his whole body of work, he will perhaps be remembered most for the musical revolution he and Parker launched. Instead of just rejecting the traditions that came before them, they re-shaped and improved them. Few instrumentalists could swing like Gillespie and Parker. At the same time, the duo pushed jazz away from being exclusively dance music to a kind that people could sit and listen to. The music they produced was more art than entertainment. It was smart, rhythmic, and absorbing. Their classic recordings are too plentiful to list here. Here is just a sampling:

"Salt Peanuts"	"Ko Ko"
"A Night in Tunisia"	"Relaxin' at Camarillo"
"Hot House"	"Parker's Mood"

The music they helped create is most often called **bebop**. Some say the name comes from a noise Charlie Christian used to mumble to himself while playing. Thelonious Monk thought it came from "Bip Bop," a song he had composed. Dizzy thought it might have come from the scat singing he used to do while calling out song numbers to his band. Not all of the musicians approved of the nickname. For example, Billy Eckstine suggested that the new sound be called "progressive jazz." Kenny Clarke preferred to keep it simple. "We never labeled the music," he said. "It was just modern music. We wouldn't call it anything, really, just music."

AFRO-CUBAN JAZZ

As we have seen, Mexican and Cuban music traditions helped shape the roots of jazz as far back as New Orleans's Congo Square. The first successful band to expand on those traditions was the Afro-Cubans, led by vocalist Francisco Grillo, known as "Machito." Cuban trumpeter Mario Bauzá and Puerto Rican trombonist Juan Tizol also added Latin style to American big-band music. Bauzá sparked Dizzy Gillespie's interest in Afro-Cuban music when both men played in the Cab Calloway Orchestra. Gillespie wanted to experiment with adding conga drums to his group. In 1947, he did just that, performing a legendary concert at Carnegie Hall with Cuban master percussionist **Chano Pozo**. The audience was thrilled by Pozo's electrifying conga solos and passionate chanting. The two men went on to compose several songs together, including "Manteca," "Tin Tin Deo," and "Guachi Guaro." Sometimes called Latin jazz, the tradition of Bauzá, Gillespie, and Pozo can also be heard in the music of Tito Puente, Mongo Santamaría, and Chucho Valdés, to name just a few.

Congas, Bongos, and Timbales
Drumming is a vital part of Afro-Cuban jazz. It usually involves three kinds of drums.

The **conga**, sometimes called the tumbadora, is a tall, narrow, single-headed drum. Conga players strike its surface with their hands. **Bongos** are a pair of small drums that fit between musicians' knees. They play them with their fingers. **Timbales**, played with sticks, are often played along with one or more cowbells.

LISTEN ALONG

Scan the QR code and click on track 9 to hear an example of Afro-Cuban jazz.

The Cool Era

While bebop was still going strong, some jazz musicians began to explore songs with slower tempos and drumming that gently coaxed the rhythm instead of urging it along. For some listeners, this restrained style boosted the emotional power of the music. Emerging in the late 1940s, this new way of playing was often described as "cool."

Miles Davis

While Charlie Parker was helping to create bebop with Dizzy Gillespie, he also started working with another trumpeter. The young man's name was Miles Davis. As a young prodigy in East St. Louis, Illinois, he grew up under the watchful eyes of his father, a dentist, and his mother, a music teacher. A friend of the family gave him a trumpet when he was 9. By high school, he was good enough to sit in with the top bands in nearby St. Louis. In 1944, he left home to study music at the Juilliard School in New York City. When he got there, he spent all his free time looking for Dizzy and Bird.

They already knew the young man. When they were touring with Billy Eckstine, the orchestra stopped in St. Louis for an engagement. When the third trumpet player got too sick to play, Miles had been invited to take his place. He played with the band for two weeks.

In New York, he got together with Parker and began to spend more time with him than at school. He dropped out in 1945 to play professionally full-time. He joined Parker's quintet in 1947. For the next forty years, Davis was one of the most important musicians in the world. If something exciting and new was happening in jazz, he was likely at the center of it.

In 1948, Miles Davis recorded an album called *Birth of the Cool*. Unusual for jazz, *Birth of the Cool* featured a nonet, or nine-piece band. Even more unusual, two of the instruments were a tuba and a French horn. The album wasn't released until 1957, but it is a highlight of the **"cool"** movement in jazz.

LISTEN ALONG

Scan the QR code and click on track 10 to hear an example of cool jazz.

▲ Miles Davis

45

"Cool" Musicians

A pianist from Canada, **Gil Evans** was one of four arrangers on *Birth of the Cool*. He went on to become one of Davis's closest musical partners. He worked with Davis on *Miles Ahead*, *Porgy and Bess*, *Sketches of Spain*, and other classic albums.

Gerry "Jeru" Mulligan was a baritone saxophonist who also arranged some of the songs on *Birth of the Cool*. He wrote his first arrangements for professional bands while still in high school. In 1952, he moved to Los Angeles, and soon formed his own quartet.

His "cool" music came to be seen as part of the West Coast style of jazz.

Lee Konitz was another musician known for cool jazz. An alto saxophonist from Chicago, he had a very long career. He played in different styles, continuing to record until he was 90 years old.

Gunther Schuller was a composer, conductor, and French horn player. The son of a violinist with the New York Philharmonic, he grew up in a musical household. At 16, he became so good at

playing the French horn that he dropped out of high school to play with the famed conductor Arturo Toscanini. He went on to play with the American Ballet Theatre and the Cincinnati Symphony Orchestra. He was principal horn player for the Metropolitan Opera orchestra when he joined the group working on *Birth of the Cool*. Schuller went on to record with other jazz musicians, including Dizzy Gillespie and Charles Mingus.

His friendship with *Birth of the Cool* pianist John Lewis led both men to start

◄ Gil Evans

a group called the Modern Jazz Society. They explored creating music that blended European musical traditions with jazz. Schuller came up with a new name for this new sound. He called it "**third stream**." Schuller went on to win a Pulitzer Prize and a MacArthur Fellowship for his work.

John Lewis had worked as a pianist and arranger for Dizzy Gillespie before doing the same work with Miles Davis. He arranged three songs on *Birth of the Cool*. In 1952 he became the leader of the acclaimed **Modern Jazz Quartet**, often celebrated for its cool sound. The group performed and recorded on and off for forty years. Its other members were vibraphonist Milt Jackson, bassist Percy Heath, and drummer Connie Kay. Their best-known song is "Bag's Groove."

Chet Baker didn't play on *Birth of the Cool*, but he is closely linked to that musical style. A vocalist as well as a trumpeter, he was a star soloist in Gerry Mulligan's quartet. He is remembered for songs such as "My Funny Valentine" and "Chetty's Lullaby."

Hard Bop and Other Sounds

LISTEN ALONG

Scan the QR code and click on track 11 to hear an example of hard bop.

While cool jazz remained a favorite style among West Coast musicians, a new sound was emerging in other parts of the country. Called "**hard bop**," it included elements found in other forms of popular Black music, such as the blues, gospel, and rhythm & blues.

▲ The Brown-Roach Quintet

The Brown-Roach Quintet

Clifford Brown, a trumpeter, and **Max Roach**, a drummer, formed a quintet in 1954 and played together until 1956. They made several albums considered classics of hard bop. Two of their notable songs included "Joy Spring" and "Delilah."

One member of the Brown-Roach Quintet went on to great fame. Born in New York City in 1930, **Sonny Rollins** started out on the alto saxophone before switching to tenor at age 16.

Still in his twenties when he joined Brown and Roach, he had already played with a number of notable musicians. These included Charlie Parker, Thelonious Monk, Miles Davis, and the Modern Jazz Quartet. His sixth album, *Saxophone Colossus*, established him as a superstar of the hard bop era.

Rollins was known for taking breaks from performing in public, even at the height of his fame. During a period of two years, he practiced every day on the Williamsburg Bridge in New York, perfecting his craft for fifteen to sixteen hours at a time. He is admired as much for his composing as for his playing. Several of his compositions are jazz standards, including "St. Thomas" and "Oleo." A list of Rollins's masterpiece albums would fill a book by itself. It would certainly include *Freedom Suite*, *Now's the Time*, and *East Broadway Run Down*.

After seven decades, including more than sixty recordings and countless concerts around the world, Rollins stopped performing in public in 2012. He is considered among the best ever to play his instrument.

Art Blakey and the Jazz Messengers

When many jazz fans think of hard bop, they think of drummer Art Blakey. His musical roots go back to the late 1930s, when he joined Fletcher Henderson's big band. He went on to play with Mary Lou Williams and Billy Eckstine. He performed for more than six decades, often as leader of the Jazz Messengers. He formed the group with Horace Silver in the mid-1950s. For the next thirty-five years, Blakey hired younger musicians as bandmates and apprentices. He mentored generations of talented artists, more than 200 in all. He also played on nearly one hundred recordings during his career, each highlighted by his explosive drumming. "Along Came Betty" and "Moanin'" are two of his best-known songs.

After forming the Jazz Messengers with Art Blakey, Silver left to start his own group with saxophonist **Hank Mobley**. A pianist and composer, Silver wrote catchy tunes that found admirers beyond the jazz world. His best-known songs include "Song for My Father" and "Peace."

Charles Mingus

Bassist, bandleader, and major American composer Charles Mingus was born in 1922 in Arizona and raised in Los Angeles. He was introduced to music in church and through listening to Duke Ellington's radio broadcasts from the Cotton Club. As a boy he took up trombone and cello before deciding on the bass in high school. From that point on, he was seldom without his instrument. Determined to be the best, he studied with experts in both jazz and European symphonic music. He also studied composition and practiced up to eighteen hours a day. At age 20, he started playing professionally in California with Louis Armstrong, Lionel Hampton, and others. About ten years later, he moved to New York. He played with important musicians such as Charlie Parker and Ellington before putting together his own bands. Whether composing or playing, he was restless and adventurous, always trying to bring out something new in the music. He recorded more than eighty albums. Mingus composed many standout songs, including "Better Git It in Your Soul," "Wednesday Night Prayer Meeting," and "Epitaph."

▸ **Charles Mingus**

Erroll Garner

Born in Pittsburgh in 1921, Garner was the youngest of six children. They all took piano lessons except for Erroll, who taught himself to play at age 3 and never learned to read music. He moved to New York in 1944 and soon became a popular performer. Audiences loved his dramatic, joyous style and the way he often hummed loudly while he played. A gifted composer, he wrote more than 300 songs, including "Misty," a jazz classic. One of the biggest-selling jazz artists of the 1950s and 1960s, he appeared regularly as a guest on television variety shows. Unlike most jazz stars of his day, Garner seldom played in nightclubs. Instead, he entertained large audiences in auditoriums and symphony halls. His legendary album *Concert by the Sea*, recorded in 1955, sold more than one million copies in three years.

Quincy Jones

Jones has been outstanding at many things, including producing pop music hits, creating Emmy-winning TV shows, and running record labels. It's easy to forget that he got his start in jazz. Born in Chicago and raised near Seattle, Jones went on the road in the 1950s. He worked as a trumpeter and arranger for Lionel Hampton and Dizzy Gillespie. In addition, he wrote arrangements for Sarah Vaughan, Count Basie, and many other popular jazz performers. He recorded his first album as a leader in 1955. In 1964, he wrote music for *The Pawnbroker*, a Hollywood film. He would go on to compose for nearly forty more. Near the end of the 1960s, he began to devote less time to jazz. But he returned to his musical roots from time to time. In 1991, he teamed up with Miles Davis for a live performance at the famous Montreux Jazz Festival. The recording made from that concert was Davis's final album. Quincy Jones's most memorable compositions include "Stockholm Sweetnin'" and "Soul Bossa Nova."

▲ **Sun Ra and the Arkestra**

Sun Ra

After leading a local band in his hometown of Birmingham, Alabama, Herman Blount moved to Chicago in 1945. He found work with Fletcher Henderson and performed briefly with Coleman Hawkins. In the mid-1950s, he changed his name to Le Sony'r Ra, called himself Sun Ra, and formed his band, the Arkestra. The band sometimes had as many as thirty members performing in flowing robes and colorful costumes.

Audiences sometimes stared in wonder as the musicians shared the stage with dancers and fire-eaters. A pianist, Sun Ra played electric piano and synthesizers years before most jazz musicians did. He recorded more than one hundred albums and led the Arkestra until 1993. His best-known songs include "Space Is the Place" and "Interplanetary Music."

NINA SIMONE

Her name was Eunice Waymon when she was growing up in Tryon, North Carolina. Born in 1933, she showed her musical gifts early by playing the piano when she was only 3 years old. She dreamed of a career in a symphony orchestra. It seemed to be close to coming true when she applied for admission to the Curtis Institute of Music in Philadelphia. Heartbroken when the school rejected her, she made her way to Atlantic City, New Jersey, where she found work as a pianist at the Midtown Bar to pay for private lessons. She changed her name to Nina Simone because she didn't want her strict parents to find out that she was performing the blues. At the Midtown Bar, she sang in public for the first time. Soon, crowds of people were flocking to the bar to see her. Her first hit song, released in 1959, made it clear that she was a special talent. With her deep, strong voice full of heartfelt emotion, she became an icon of Black pride. Few were better at singing romantic ballads, and even fewer could equal her ability to sing a fiery song calling for change. Over four decades, she recorded more than forty original albums. Her best tunes include "Feeling Good," "Four Women," and "To Be Young, Gifted, and Black."

All-Star Lineup

In the late 1950s, Miles Davis put together a group often referred to as his first great quintet. Miles was better than most at recognizing talented musicians to work with. His bandmates were: Red Garland (piano), Paul Chambers (bass), Philly Joe Jones (drums), and Sonny Rollins (tenor saxophone, later replaced by John Coltrane, whom we will meet again soon). Sometimes they were joined by a sixth musician, Julian "Cannonball" Adderley (alto saxophone). Their classic recordings include *Milestones* and *'Round About Midnight*.

▲ **Miles Davis and the First Great Quintet**

Lambert, Hendricks & Ross

Dave Lambert, John Hendricks, and Annie Ross got together in 1957, and for the next six years were one of the most popular jazz vocal groups in the United States. Their album *Sing a Song of Basie* was the first of several hit recordings. They specialized in **vocalese**, a style of jazz singing in which a vocalist adds words to an instrumental song.

VOCALESE

. . . .

Vocalese is different from scat singing because it uses actual words, often sung speedily, instead of pure sounds. These are three of the best vocalese singers:

Eddie Jefferson

King Pleasure

Al Jarreau

A Great Day in Harlem

On August 12, 1958, a photographer named Art Kane gathered fifty-seven of the greatest living jazz artists for a group photo. It included many of the musicians we've met in these pages, including Dizzy Gillespie, Thelonious Monk, and Sonny Rollins. Because jazz musicians often work late at night, they seldom wake up early. Yet they assembled at ten o'clock in the morning, and they didn't mind. "It was sheer happiness," said bassist Milt Hinton. "It was like a family reunion," recalled saxophonist Johnny Griffin, "being in one spot with all these great jazz musicians at one time." The photo, known as *A Great Day in Harlem*, or *Harlem 1958*, became world famous after appearing in a 1959 issue of *Esquire* magazine entitled *The Golden Age of Jazz*.

In 1994, filmmaker Jean Bach made a documentary about the historical event called *A Great Day in Harlem*. Since then, similar group photos have taken their names from this image. For example, there are notable photos called "A Great Day in Hip-Hop" and "A Great Day in Doo-Wop."

▲ Photographer Art Kane setting up for the *Great Day in Harlem* photograph

JAZZ AT THE MOVIES

In the late 1950s, moviemakers began to call on the finest composers in jazz to bring their talents to the big screen.

Elevator to the Gallows (1958)

Miles Davis wrote original music for this French film about love and war. After watching scenes from the movie, he'd work out ideas on the piano in his Paris hotel room.

Shadows (1958)

Charles Mingus wrote several songs for this film about two struggling African American jazz musicians and their sister. When the film was revised in 1959, nearly all of his songs were taken out.

Anatomy of a Murder (1959)

Duke Ellington composed the score for this mystery starring Jimmy Stewart. He even appears in one scene as a pianist named Pie Eye.

KIND OF BLUE

In 1959, Miles Davis recorded *Kind of Blue*, considered by many to be the greatest jazz album ever made. It has sold more than five million copies, and is even treasured by music fans who seldom choose jazz. The six songs on the record include "All Blues" and "So What," which has become a beloved standard. Davis's band members included Coltrane, Adderley, and newcomer **Bill Evans**, a pianist. Evans went on to achieve success as a composer, solo artist, and leader of his own trio. His best-known compositions include "Peace Piece" and "Waltz for Debby."

Cannonball Adderley's big break came as a sideman for Miles Davis. For Adderley's first album as a leader, Davis returned the favor. In addition to playing the trumpet, Davis composed the title song, "Somethin' Else." The son of two college professors, Adderley worked as a high school music teacher in Florida before moving to New York City in 1955. After leaving Davis's group, he went on to lead a successful quintet with his brother Nat, a cornetist. "Mercy, Mercy, Mercy" and "Work Song" are among his best-known songs.

▲ Miles Davis, John Coltrane, and Cannonball Adderley

Take Five

Born in 1920, **Dave Brubeck** grew up on a large farm in Ione, California. His mother didn't allow him or his two brothers to listen to the radio, but she did give them permission to make music of their own. Piano was Dave's choice. In 1959 he teamed up with alto saxophonist **Paul Desmond** to record one of the most popular jazz albums in history: *Time Out* sold more than two million copies. One song from the album, "Take Five," even made the pop charts.

The Sidewinder

Born in Philadelphia in 1938, **Lee Morgan** was given his first trumpet at age 13. By age 18 he was good enough to join Dizzy Gillespie's big band. The next fifteen years were very productive for Morgan. He played with John Coltrane, Art Blakey, and many more big names before leading his own band. His album *Candy*, released in 1958, is considered a classic of hard bop. In 1964, he composed and performed *The Sidewinder*, which became a surprise hit on the pop charts.

TOOTING THEIR HORNS

There was no shortage of great trumpet players during the hard bop era. Here are three more.

Art Farmer

Freddie Hubbard

Clark Terry

The Golden Age of Pianists

Someone described the 1960s as a "golden age" of pianists. It was certainly a fruitful time for **Oscar Peterson**. The Canadian-born pianist had been a star since the 1940s, noted for his flying fingers and joyous, swinging approach to the keyboard. In 1962, he had one of the biggest hit albums in his career, a jazzed-up version of music from the popular Broadway play, *West Side Story*. Over the course of sixty years, he recorded more than 200 albums in nearly every setting—with big bands, as part of a trio, playing solo, and accompanying vocalists like Billie Holiday and Ella Fitzgerald.

Pittsburgh is the place where several great pianists grew up. Erroll Garner, Mary Lou Williams, and Billy Strayhorn are three of them. **Ahmad Jamal** is a fourth. Born in

1930, he began playing at age 3 and started formal lessons at 7. He moved to Chicago in 1950, where he soon formed his own trio. His 1958 album, *At the Pershing: But Not for Me*, became a bestseller, staying on the charts for 108 weeks. It remains one of the most popular jazz albums of all time. One song from the album, "Poinciana," is Jamal's most recognized tune.

As the 1950s turned into the 1960s, jazz artists continued to make classic hard bop recordings. They also began to experiment with other musical styles. **Cecil Taylor**'s music didn't sound like the kind of jazz most people were used to. Some jazz fans and musicians did not like his improvisations. Others thought they were too difficult to enjoy. None of that discouraged Taylor. Born

in Queens, New York, in 1929, he fell in love with the piano when he was a young boy. He practiced six days a week. Later he trained at New England Conservatory in Boston, where he developed a deep knowledge of many kinds of music. By the time his second album, *Looking Ahead!*, was released in 1956, he had become known for his unique compositions and dramatic performance style. At concerts, he sometimes got up from the piano to recite original poetry. He won many prizes over the course of his long career. He lived to influence many pianists who came after him. "Bemsha Swing" and "Wallering" are good songs for listeners meeting his music for the first time.

Talented saxophonists were plentiful. These were three of the best:

Benny Golson, tenor

Hank Mobley, tenor

Jackie McLean, alto

John Coltrane

Remember when we met the members of Miles Davis's first great quintet? Let's get re-acquainted with one of them. A tenor and soprano saxophonist, John Coltrane went on to create a compelling and highly praised body of work. In addition to working with Miles Davis, he had played with other jazz standouts, most notably pianist Thelonious Monk. From 1962 to 1965, he may have been the biggest star in jazz. His albums during this period include *My Favorite Things*, *Ballads*, and *Impressions*. *A Love Supreme*, recorded in 1964, is widely regarded as a masterpiece. During this period, Coltrane led his "classic" quartet:

Elvin Jones (drums)

McCoy Tyner (piano)

Jimmy Garrison (bass)

A restless artist who liked to experiment, Coltrane was constantly searching for new ways to express himself, even at the risk of leaving some of his followers behind. Years after his death in 1967, no conversation about jazz is complete without mention of his work. By any measure, Coltrane was one of the most significant musicians of the twentieth century.

▲ John Coltrane

Free Jazz

In 1959, **Ornette Coleman** released an album called *The Shape of Jazz to Come*. The following year, he released another one called *Free Jazz*. With those two recordings, he demonstrated new ways of thinking about and playing jazz. In time, Coleman came to call his new method **harmolodics**, a word composed from harmony, movement, and melody. Some jazz musicians and listeners didn't like Coleman's sound when they first heard it. Many of them began to think better of it after hearing it more often. By the end of his career, Coleman had become one of the most important jazz musicians of his time.

A composer and alto saxophonist from Fort Worth, Texas, Coleman got his start playing in Southern R&B bands. His next stop was Los Angeles, where he spent six years shaping his sound. He then settled in New York. By the time he retired from playing in 2014, he had been awarded a Pulitzer Prize and a MacArthur Fellowship. The other members of his groundbreaking quartet were Don Cherry (trumpet), Charlie Haden (bass), and Billy Higgins (drums).

Keeping Up with the Joneses

Detroit and the towns surrounding it have been long known as the birthplaces of talented jazz artists. It was even possible to find more than one in a single household. Perhaps the best example of this bounty is the Jones brothers of Pontiac, Michigan.

Elvin Jones

The youngest of the three brothers, Elvin is best known for his important role in Coltrane's quartet. He also played with many other musicians, including Sonny Rollins, Miles Davis, and Charles Mingus. Born in 1927, he was drawn to percussion from an early age. As a child he would beat pots and pans with a wooden spoon in his mother's kitchen. He began to teach himself when he was 13, but couldn't afford his own drum kit until he left the army in 1949. As leader of his own band, the Elvin Jones Jazz Machine, he mentored many younger musicians, including Joshua Redman and Nicholas Payton.

Thad Jones

Born in 1923, Thad was the middle brother of the three. Like his brother Elvin, he was mostly self-taught. A cornetist and trumpeter, composer, arranger, and bandleader, he was in the Count Basie Orchestra for four years. During that time, he contributed many arrangements and original compositions. In 1963, he went out on his own to work as an arranger. Two years later, he formed a big band with drummer Mel Lewis. The orchestra was successful for twelve years, winning a Grammy Award in 1978 and much acclaim. He moved to Copenhagen, Denmark, in 1979, where he took over the Danish Radio Big Band. He came back to the United States in 1985 to lead the Count Basie Orchestra after Basie's death. But he soon became ill and returned to Copenhagen, where he died in 1986. "A Child Is Born" is his best-known composition.

▲ Hank Jones, Elvin Jones, and Thad Jones

Hank Jones

The eldest of the three brothers, Hank was born in 1918. One of the most respected pianists of his generation, he may be best known for his work with Ella Fitzgerald. He performed with her for six years, but also found time to work with Charlie Parker and others. After Fitzgerald, he worked as a background musician in film and television for many years. He also performed with several trios and was musical director for *Ain't Misbehavin'*, a Broadway musical inspired by Fats Waller. A very busy studio musician, he worked as a sideman on more than 1,000 albums.

AND THE WINNER IS . . .

Presented every year, the Grammy Awards are among the most prestigious honors available to musical artists. They are sponsored by the National Academy of Recording Arts and Sciences (NARAS). Its members are musicians, producers, and other professionals who work in the recording industry. The winner is chosen from ten nominees in each category, including jazz, rock, and R&B. Each winner receives a trophy in the shape of a golden gramophone, an early version of a record player. Today there are more than eighty categories, but at the first Grammy ceremony in 1959 there were just twenty-eight. Jazz musicians Count Basie and Ella Fitzgerald were among the winners.

Jazz in South Africa

In January 1960, six of the greatest jazz musicians in South Africa met in a studio in Johannesburg. They recorded *Jazz Epistle Verse 1*, the first jazz album by an all-Black South African band. Soon after, the South African government cracked down on its citizens, reinforcing its policy of racial separation. Jazz was banned from the radio and activists were threatened with punishment. The country was no longer safe, perhaps especially for creative artists. Two members of the band eventually made their way to the United States, where they became prominent members of the jazz scene.

Abdullah Ibrahim, a pianist and composer, arrived in New York City in the mid-1960s. He had been encouraged to make the move by Duke Ellington, who had heard him play in Zurich, Switzerland. He helped him get signed to an American record label. Since then, Ibrahim has recorded almost seventy albums. In his compositions, he has often strived to highlight the link between jazz and modern African music.

Songs to listen to: "Mannenberg," "Water from an Ancient Well"

Hugh Masekela, a trumpeter, moved to New York City in 1960. With the help of singers Harry Belafonte and Miriam Makeba, he received a scholarship to the Manhattan School of Music. Outside of school, he visited nightclubs where Charles Mingus, Max Roach, and other legends performed. One night he met Miles Davis. He advised Masekela to avoid imitating his heroes and instead develop his own sound. Taking Davis's words to heart, he created a blend of jazz and *mbaqanga*, a musical style from his homeland. By 1968, he had recorded a hit single, "Grazing in the Grass." It stayed at the top of the American charts for three weeks. By the time of his death in 2018, Masekela had recorded more than forty albums. He played with a variety of top musicians, including reggae star Bob Marley and Nigerian bandleader Fela Kuti.

Songs to listen to: "Grazing in the Grass," "Soweto Blues"

▲ The Jazz Epistles

▲ Stan Getz

Stan Getz and Bossa Nova

As a high school student in the Bronx, Stan Getz was chosen for the all-city orchestra. Offered a chance to study at the Juilliard School, the young tenor saxophonist turned it down. Instead, he went on the road to become a working jazz musician. By the 1950s, he had become a respected bandmate with a sound all his own. Along the way, he played with a range of notable instrumentalists, including Benny Goodman and Max Roach. A proven master of many styles, Getz had a huge hit in 1962, when

pop hits for jazz musicians rarely happened. With guitarist Charlie Byrd he recorded *Jazz Samba*. An album of Brazilian tunes, it became the first instrumental jazz album to reach number one on the Billboard pop charts. It sold half a million copies within eighteen months and introduced Getz to a new set of admirers.

Jazz Samba launched an American craze for **bossa nova**, a musical style first created by Brazilian musicians in the 1950s. Bossa nova is Portuguese for "new beat" or

"new thing." Its sound contains elements of samba, an Afro-Brazilian music style, and cool jazz. Some of the first bossa nova musicians included composers Antônio Carlos Jobim, Luiz Bonfa, and João Gilberto. In 1964, Stan Getz recorded a landmark album with several of these musicians, which won the Grammy Award for Album of the Year. *Getz/Gilberto* includes perhaps the best-known bossa nova song, "The Girl from Ipanema," sung by Astrud Gilberto.

Miles Davis and the Second Great Quintet

In 1963, Miles Davis put together the group now known as his Second Great Quintet. It included pianist Herbie Hancock, Tony Williams on drums, Ron Carter on bass, and saxophonist Wayne Shorter, who joined later. Their albums include *E.S.P.*, *Nefertiti*, and *Sorcerer*. **Ron Carter** went on to become the most recorded bassist of all time. He has appeared on more than 2,200 recording sessions, including dates with soul artists Roberta Flack and Aretha Franklin, as well as the hip-hop group A Tribe Called Quest.

Herbie Hancock had already produced a hit album of his own before joining forces with Miles Davis. *Takin' Off*, released in 1962, had featured a hit single, "Watermelon Man." It was the first of many triumphs, and not only in jazz. Over the course of more than fifty years, Hancock would know

success in many different forms of music.

Born in Chicago in 1940, he seemed destined for fame at an early age. He played a Mozart concerto with the Chicago Symphony when he was just 11. At Grinnell College, he studied music and electrical engineering before heading to Chicago in 1960. He first began to play electric piano while working with Davis. He continued his interest in electric and electronic instruments when he went out on his own. In 1973, with his new band, the Headhunters, Hancock played synthesizers in addition to electric piano. The group's first album, *Head Hunters*, mixing jazz with rock, funk, and R&B, was at that time the best-selling jazz record ever. For most of his career, Hancock has played both traditional jazz and music that blends different styles. In 1983, his hit single, "Rockit,"

won a Grammy for best R&B Instrumental Performance. He has won fourteen Grammys in all, including one for Album of the Year in 2008. He also won an Oscar in 1987 for scoring *'Round Midnight*, a movie starring saxophone great Dexter Gordon.

Wayne Shorter had been music director of Art Blakey's Jazz Messengers before leaving to join Davis's quintet. He is widely admired for his work on soprano and tenor saxophone, although he may be even more acclaimed as a composer. During his six years with Davis, he wrote several of the quintet's most notable songs, including "E.S.P.," "Footprints," and "Prince of Darkness." Shorter's own acclaimed albums include *Speak No Evil* and *Native Dancer*. He also became an important figure in the development of fusion, which we'll learn more about in just a bit.

▲ **Miles Davis and the Second Great Quintet**

Rahsaan Roland Kirk

Sightless since age 2, **Rahsaan Roland Kirk** studied saxophone at the Ohio School for the Blind. As a teenager he found work with a traveling R&B band. He quickly gained attention for his amazing ability to play three saxophones at once, but Kirk is remembered today not just because of this unbelievable feat. He was a gifted improviser, arranger, and bandleader as well. He had a deep knowledge of various musical styles, including blues and stride piano. A master of multiple instruments, he also played harmonica, flute, clarinet, and English horn. Throughout the 1960s and much of the 1970s, he was highly praised for both his recordings and his live performances. His notable albums include *Introducing Roland Kirk* and *We Free Kings*.

The Organists

During the 1950s and 1960s, music featuring the Hammond B-3 organ was in high demand. Unlike the traditional organ, which relies on pipes, original Hammonds were electric and used something called tone wheels. The wheels spun, creating an electric current. Each organ weighed about 425 pounds and was accompanied by a 200-pound speaker. The Hammond B-3 got a boost in 1956, when **Jimmy Smith** emerged as a star. He combined elements of blues, R&B, and gospel in a style often called **soul jazz**. His most popular songs include "The Sermon" and "Back at the Chicken Shack." Other notable organists included **Shirley Scott**, **Brother Jack McDuff**, and **Dr. Lonnie Smith**.

The Jazz Guitar

When he was 20 and working as a welder in Indianapolis, **Wes Montgomery** bought a six-string guitar. Practicing after work each day, he taught himself to play. Without learning to read music, he soon became good enough to perform in clubs. In 1948, vibraphonist Lionel Hampton hired him to join his band. The job didn't provide the big break that he thought it would, and he returned to Indianapolis. He didn't receive his own recording contract until 1959. His second album, released in 1960, convinced many listeners that Montgomery was the greatest jazz guitarist since Charlie Christian. Unlike most guitarists, he plucked the strings with the side of his thumb instead of a pick. This and other techniques helped him develop a sound like no other guitarist. Montgomery's career ended with his death in 1968. The songs he left behind include many classics, including "Bumpin' on Sunset" and "Four on Six."

Other notable jazz guitarists during the 1960s include **Grant Green** and **George Benson.**

▶ Wes Montgomery

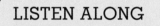

LISTEN ALONG

Scan the QR code and click on track 12 to hear the jazz guitar.

Eric Dolphy

A native of Los Angeles, Dolphy arrived in New York City in 1960 and soon joined forces with Charles Mingus. He played on several of the bassist-bandleader's albums, played live with his sextet, and toured Europe with him. By then Dolphy was known as a complete musician who could play several instruments equally well. They included alto saxophone, bass clarinet, and flute. He also played with Ornette Coleman, Gunther Schuller, and others, although it's his collaborations with John Coltrane that have gotten the most attention. At first, some listeners disliked these albums, including *Village Vanguard* and *Africa/Brass*, but they are now highly regarded. Dolphy's music as a leader started out closer to hard bop before moving into free jazz territory. *Out to Lunch!*, released in 1964, is considered his masterwork. He died later that year.

FLAUTISTS

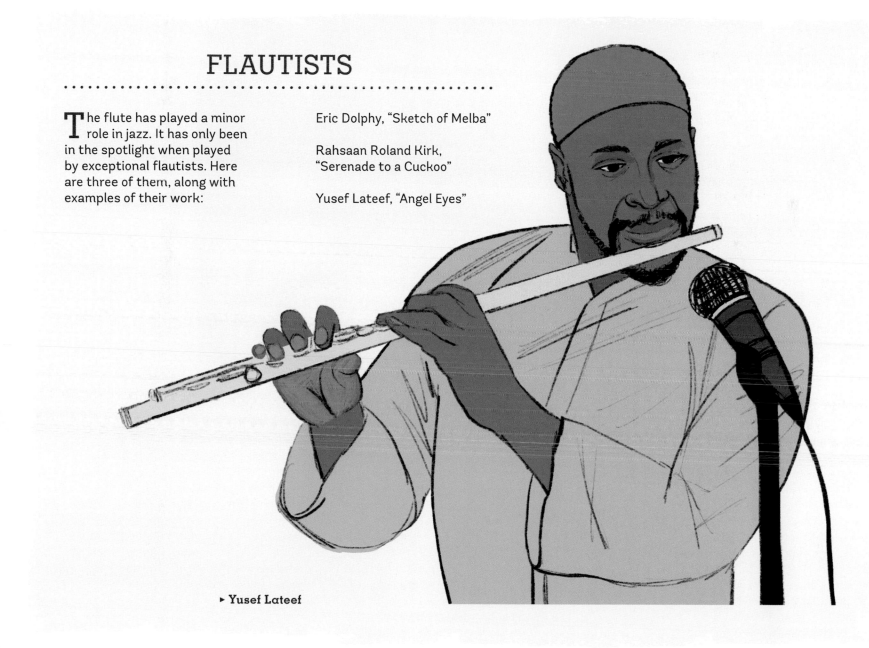

The flute has played a minor role in jazz. It has only been in the spotlight when played by exceptional flautists. Here are three of them, along with examples of their work:

Eric Dolphy, "Sketch of Melba"

Rahsaan Roland Kirk, "Serenade to a Cuckoo"

Yusef Lateef, "Angel Eyes"

▶ Yusef Lateef

Great Black Music

Like Ornette Coleman and Cecil Taylor, many musicians in the early 1960s were committed to pushing their art in new directions. They challenged old ideas about how music should be created and performed. The compositions and recordings that resulted have often been called **free jazz**. As noted earlier, people have seldom agreed on what to call different kinds of music. The members of the Association for the Advancement of Creative Musicians (AACM) prefer the term **Great Black Music**.

The AACM was founded in Chicago in 1965 by four musicians, Muhal Richard Abrams (piano), Jodie Christian (piano), Steve McCall (drums), and Phil Cohran (trumpet). Since then, dozens of artists have been associated with the group. It opened a branch in New York and expanded its renown around the world. For more than fifty years, the AACM has been open to experimentation and encouraged the composition of original music. In addition, it has always supported community engagement. Since the 1960s, its members

have operated a school where they provide free music training for young people.

AACM members have earned nearly every kind of recognition that artists can receive. Anthony Braxton (saxophonist/composer) and George E. Lewis (trombonist/composer) have been awarded fellowships from the MacArthur Foundation. Henry Threadgill, a saxophonist, flautist, and composer, has won a Pulitzer Prize.

Art Ensemble of Chicago

Some members of the AACM formed smaller groups while staying connected to the larger collective. One such group was the Art Ensemble of Chicago, founded in the late 1960s. Its original lineup consisted of trumpeter Lester Bowie, saxophonists Joseph Jarman and Roscoe Mitchell, bassist Malachi Favors, and drummer Famoudou Don Moye. They added a bit of theater to their performances by wearing elaborate costumes and face paint. In addition to traditional instruments, they played kazoos, bells, and toy instruments, showing that music could be made from almost anything.

Showcasing their unique sound around the world, they made music with artists from Africa, Asia, and Europe. Their standout albums include *A Jackson in Your House* and *Fanfare for the Warriors*.

Coltrane's Legacy

Albert Ayler

At its best, Albert Ayler's music mixes the high-energy fearlessness of free jazz with the deep emotional richness of the church music he grew up with. A native of Shaker Heights, Ohio, Ayler moved to New York City in 1963. He had been living in Europe for five years. While there, he perfected a honking tone on his tenor saxophone, a sound that even included screeching. To some listeners, his music sounded out of control and disturbing. He found some notable admirers in New York, including John Coltrane. He helped Ayler obtain a record deal and encouraged his efforts to reach a wider audience. Several albums Ayler made are considered classic examples of free jazz. They include *In Greenwich Village* and *My Name Is Albert Ayler*.

Archie Shepp

A tenor saxophonist, Archie Shepp was born in Fort Lauderdale, Florida, in 1937. He grew up in Philadelphia, acquiring his first tenor saxophone at age 15. After majoring in playwriting in college, he moved to New York City in the early 1960s to pursue a career in theater. Frustrated by the lack of opportunity, he turned to music. He found his first professional job playing with pianist Cecil Taylor. He was mentored by John Coltrane and played with him on Coltrane's album *Ascension*. In his solo work, he was at the forefront of Black composers making music that reflected their African origins and concern with civil rights. He continued to write plays, some staged off-Broadway, and became one of the first jazz musicians to become a tenured professor. He has recorded nearly one hundred albums over the course of sixty years. *Fire Music* and *Attica Blues* are among his standouts.

Pharoah Sanders

Tenor saxophonist Pharoah Sanders was yet another young musician who benefited from John Coltrane's guidance. Born in Little Rock, Arkansas, in 1940, he played clarinet in church as a child. He took up the saxophone in high school and was introduced to jazz. After graduation, he played professionally in Oakland, California, before making his way to New York City. In 1965, he met Coltrane and began a fruitful musical partnership. He played on several of his mentor's albums from his free jazz period, including *Ascension*, *Meditations*, and *Kulu Sé Mama*. As a solo artist, he has produced many masterworks, including the albums *Karma* and *Jewels of Thought*. He is perhaps best known for the song "The Creator Has a Master Plan."

▲ Albert Ayler

Alice Coltrane

John Coltrane's most important musical partner likely was his wife, Alice. A pianist, harpist, and composer, she worked closely with him on several of his late-career albums. Born in Detroit in 1937, she was encouraged by her father to pursue a life in music. She played in local clubs before moving to Paris in the late 1950s. After studying and performing there, she returned to the Detroit music scene. She met Coltrane soon after and married him in 1965. A year later, she joined his band as pianist. She recorded with him on *Expression*, *Live in Japan*, and other albums. After her husband's death in 1967, she became a bandleader herself and recorded nearly two dozen albums.

Like many women musicians, she was respected for her work but still didn't receive all the credit she deserved. In the years since her death in 2007, the number of her admirers continues to grow. Her best-known recordings include *Cosmic Music* and *Transcendence*.

Meet These Singers: Carter, Lincoln, and McRae

Betty Carter was a respected jazz veteran since the late 1940s, known for her mellow voice and impressive scat singing. She enjoyed renewed success after Miles Davis suggested that she and singer Ray Charles work together. Their popular 1961 duet album shows both vocalists at their best. She embraced the new spirit of independence among jazz artists when she started her own record label in 1969. She operated Bet-Car Records for the next eighteen years. "Mean to Me" and "Spring Can Really Hang You Up the Most" are good Betty Carter songs to begin with.

Chicago-born **Abbey Lincoln** was known for her fiery vocals and social activism. She was also an actress, co-starring in the acclaimed 1964 movie *Nothing But a Man*. She recorded more than two dozen albums from 1957 to 1990. A highlight is *We Insist!: Max Roach's Freedom Now Suite*, recorded in 1960 with drummer Max Roach. It combines vocals, poetry, and captivating music.

Carmen McRae, born in Harlem in 1920, was a piano player and chorus girl at Minton's Playhouse, where bebop was born. Her recording career began in the 1950s and continued for the next forty years. Influenced by Billie Holiday, she had a smooth voice and paid respectful attention to lyrics. Her best work includes a series of duets with Betty Carter, including such songs as "Stolen Moments," and another with Sammy Davis Jr., featuring "People Will Say We're in Love" and other tunes.

▲ Betty Carter, Carmen McRae, and Abbey Lincoln

OSCAR BROWN JR.

Singer, songwriter, storyteller—Oscar Brown Jr. is hard to describe with just one word. As a singer, he made a splashy start in 1961 when he appeared at New York City's the Village Vanguard, a popular jazz club. As a lyricist, he added words to instrumental standards such as Miles Davis's "All Blues." He also wrote lyrics for Max Roach and Abbey Lincoln's epic album, *We Insist!*. His original compositions were covered by Mahalia Jackson and other musical greats.

But these were just a few of his accomplishments. One of his plays reached Broadway in 1969 when boxing champ Muhammad Ali starred in his musical *Buck White*. On television, he hosted two shows about Black music, *Jazz Scene USA* and *From Jump Street*. From the beginnings of his career to its end in 2005, he devoted much of his creative energy to jazz. Celebrated as a dynamic live performer, he is also remembered for the nine albums he recorded. They include *Sin & Soul* and *Tells It Like It Is!*

Jazz Fusion

By the end of the 1960s, rock and roll was becoming very popular, pushing jazz and other forms of music aside. Some musicians embraced this change, working some elements of the new sound into their own projects. Some of their recordings sounded more like rock than jazz, while others sounded more like jazz than rock. This music is known as **fusion**. Here are some musicians who were active during this period, and some of the music they created.

▲ Miles Davis

In a Silent Way

As always, Miles Davis was among the first to spot new trends. After listening to such popular musicians as James Brown, Jimi Hendrix, and Sly and the Family Stone, he recorded *In A Silent Way* (1969). That album and the one that followed a year later featured electronic keyboards, electric bass, and beats borrowed from rock and roll. Musicians involved in those projects included Chick Corea and Herbie Hancock (electric piano), Tony Williams (drums), Joe Zawinul (electric piano and organ), Dave Holland (double bass), and John McLaughlin (electric guitar). Most of them went on to lead successful fusion efforts of their own.

Tony Williams was just 17 when he joined Davis's Second Great Quintet in 1963. By then he'd already been playing professionally for four years. In 1969 he formed his own band, the Tony Williams Lifetime, with John McLaughlin and organist Larry Young. The group didn't stay together long, and Williams went on to other ventures. Still, their first album, *Emergency!,* is considered an example of fusion at its best.

◄ Miles Davis with a jazz fusion band

The Godfather of Fusion

Larry Coryell was one of the first gifted jazz instrumentalists to welcome the influence of rock, and he is sometimes called the "godfather of fusion." His life changed, he said, when he heard a Wes Montgomery record. Soon he was teaching himself to play along. He arrived in New York City from Washington State in 1965. Five years later, he recorded a breakthrough album, *Spaces*. During the 1970s, the golden age of fusion, he recorded more than twenty albums. He released more than sixty albums in all, including several with his famous fusion band, The Eleventh House.

Songs to listen to: "Birdfingers" and "Wrong Is Right"

▸ **Larry Coryell**

Mahavishnu Orchestra

After partnerships with Miles Davis and Tony Williams, John McLaughlin formed this band in 1971. The first lineup lasted until 1974. Later that year, McLaughlin revived the band with new members. Both groups were admired for their live performances mixing jazz, rock, and Indian classical music. Their albums include *The Inner Mounting Flame* and *Birds of Fire*.

Return to Forever

Chick Corea was a highly praised pianist who had worked with Stan Getz and Cab Calloway before playing a key role in Miles Davis's groundbreaking fusion efforts. He had also been a bandleader, having recorded at least one classic album, *Now He Sings, Now He Sobs*. In 1972, he formed the band Return to Forever. After bassist Stanley Clarke, drummer Lenny White, and electric guitarist Al Di Meola joined, it became one of the most celebrated bands of its time. Corea, a master of any form of jazz he tried, won twenty-five Grammy Awards. He was also a first-rate composer. "Spain" and "Crystal Silence" are just two of his many standards.

▸ **Chick Corea**

Weather Report

This band was founded in 1970 by keyboardist Joe Zawinul, saxophonist Wayne Shorter, and bassist Miroslav Vitouš. It members changed often during its sixteen-year run, most notably when **Jaco Pastorius** became its bassist in 1976. The group never limited itself to fusion. Its songs also included funk, R&B, and world music trends. Still, many jazz fans regard it as the best fusion band ever.

Songs to listen to: "Birdland," "River People"

Head Hunters

Like many top fusion bands, Head Hunters was formed by a musician who had played with Miles Davis. Herbie Hancock, whom we met earlier, founded the group in 1973. Its first album, mixing jazz, funk, and rock, sold more than one million copies. "Chameleon" was the band's biggest hit.

Pat Metheny

Guitarist Pat Metheny was so good that he taught music at two colleges while still in his late teens. He is admired on both acoustic and electric guitar. A fan of Miles Davis and Wes Montgomery, he first appeared on an album in 1974 with Jaco Pastorius as leader. Two years later, at age 21, he released his first album, *Bright Size Life*. Working often with keyboardist Lyle Mays, he has recorded songs that have made both the jazz and pop charts. He has won twenty Grammy Awards.

▲ **Head Hunters Band**

75

Keith Jarrett

Keith Jarrett spent part of his early career playing fusion. He played electric organ and electric piano on several Miles Davis albums from the fusion era. He quickly returned to the acoustic piano and went on to greater fame. Jarrett left the Davis band in 1971. In 1973 he performed a series of recitals showcasing his brilliant talent for improvisation. An album recorded at a 1975 performance, *The Köln Concert*, is considered a masterpiece. It's also one of the best-selling solo piano albums of all time. Although he continued to present solo concerts throughout his career, he didn't always play alone. He also led successful quartets in Europe and the United States.

The Godfather of Rap

Because he often recited highly musical rhymes, **Gil Scott-Heron** has been called the "godfather of rap." A poet and musician like no other, he felt a much closer connection to jazz. Born in Chicago and raised in Tennessee and New York, he published his first novel when he was 19. His second came a year later. In 1970 he turned to music, singing and chanting his lyrics to the accompaniment of percussion. On later albums, he worked with jazz musicians such as bassist Ron Carter and Brian Jackson, a flautist and keyboardist. Few artists have combined jazz rhythms and lyrics calling for change as skillfully as Scott-Heron. His best work includes "The Revolution Will Not Be Televised," "Lady Day and John Coltrane," and "Johannesburg."

▲ The Toshiko Akiyoshi Jazz Orchestra featuring Lew Tabackin

The Toshiko Akiyoshi–Lew Tabackin Big Band

During a time when most jazz musicians were trying to save money by working in small groups, Toshiko Akiyoshi and Lew Tabackin did just the opposite. In 1973, the married couple formed a sixteen-piece ensemble. They were based in Los Angeles for the first nine years of the band's existence. Then they moved to New York and changed the group's name to **The Toshiko Akiyoshi Jazz Orchestra featuring Lew Tabackin**. They continued to perform and tour until 2003. They recorded twenty-three albums and received multiple Grammy nominations. Throughout that time, Akiyoshi, a pianist, arranged all the music and composed nearly all the songs. Tabackin played tenor saxophone and flute. Born in the Manchurian region of China in 1929, Akiyoshi returned with her family to occupied Japan after World War II. In 1952, she was discovered by the great pianist Oscar Peterson, who helped her get a recording contract. She came to the U.S. to study at the Berklee School of Music, where she was the first Japanese student to enroll.

Songs to listen to: "Strive for Jive," "Harvest Shuffle"

World Saxophone Quartet

One of the more inventive groups during this period was the World Saxophone Quartet. Deciding to perform without support from drums, bass, or piano, they formed the quartet in 1976. Oliver Lake, Julius Hemphill, Hamiet Bluett, and David Murray could each play multiple instruments, but their lineup usually featured two altos, one tenor, and a baritone saxophone. Their lively concerts featured their original compositions but also included selections from the Ellington and Motown songbooks, as well as familiar R&B hits. "Steppin'" and "Night Train" are good examples of the quartet's range and skill.

Marian McPartland

Remember the historic photo *A Great Day in Harlem*? Marian McPartland was one of the few women seen on camera that morning in 1958. A pianist and composer who'd come to New York from England in 1946, she found steady work and had her songs covered by Sarah Vaughan and others. It was the beginning of a promising career. But she was just getting started, going on to launch her own record label in 1969. And, at a time when many lives in show business were slowing down, hers picked up unexpectedly. In 1978, she became the host of *Piano Jazz*, a public radio show. On each show, she interviewed jazz musicians while playing duets with them. The show became enormously popular and aired on more than 200 radio stations around the world. By the time McPartland stepped down in 2011, *Piano Jazz* had become the longest-running show of its kind.

▸ **Marian McPartland**

The Eclectic Era

Interest in fusion faded as jazz musicians and their audiences turned again toward acoustic instruments. This doesn't mean that everyone gave up on fusion, or that everyone had adopted it in the first place. The new era was sometimes called neo-bop or neo-traditional, but neither is entirely correct. Even musicians who called for a return to earlier methods remained open to new ways of composing and playing. It may make sense to call it the **eclectic** era (*eclectic* means borrowing from a broad range of sources), or the "age of anything goes." Since the end of the twentieth century, musicians have felt at liberty to reflect any part of the jazz tradition, from Dixieland to free jazz. They also continue to make room in their compositions for funk, rock, hip-hop, and other kinds of music.

▲ The RH Factor band

Wynton Marsalis

His first album, released in 1982 when he was 19 years old, marked the arrival of a new generation of jazz musicians. A trumpeter, composer, and bandleader, Marsalis has spoken often about the importance of honoring the history and fundamentals of the music. Born in New Orleans in 1961, he grew up in a musical household and met jazz legends such as Miles Davis when he was a small boy. He studied briefly at the Juilliard School before touring as a professional, first with Art Blakey, then with Herbie Hancock. After forming his own band in 1982, he went on to perform around 120 concerts every year for fifteen straight years. In 1983 he won Grammy Awards for jazz and European symphonic music, the first person to do so. He achieved another first for jazz musicians when he won a Pulitzer Prize in 1997 for his composition *Blood on the Fields*. He co-founded Jazz at Lincoln Center, of which he has served as artistic director since 1997. The New York–based center presents concerts, workshops, and other activities throughout the year. He has recorded more than fifty jazz albums and sold more than seven million copies worldwide. Well-known beyond the world of jazz, Marsalis is recognized as a vital musician and thinker.

Music to listen to: "Black Codes," *Swing Symphony*.

All in the Family

Wynton is the second son of **Ellis Marsalis Jr.**, who was a respected pianist and teacher.

Ellis was most proud of his work as an educator. In addition to teaching his sons, he taught trumpeters Terence Blanchard and Nicholas Payton, as well as many others. He also worked as a music professor at Virginia Commonwealth University and the University of New Orleans. As a musician, he performed with Cannonball Adderley and other greats. He recorded more than twenty albums in his career.

Branford Marsalis, eldest son of Ellis, is among the most acclaimed saxophonists of his generation. He is equally skilled on alto, soprano, and tenor saxophone. He has performed and toured with rock stars such as Sting, the Dave Matthews Band, and the Grateful Dead. He has worked with hip-hop artists too, including DJ Premier and Public Enemy. He has been touring and recording with his own quartet since 1986. In demand for his mastery of European symphonic music, he has been a featured soloist with various international orchestras. In 1992, he became the first African American musical director on late-night TV when he led the orchestra of *The Tonight Show with Jay Leno*. He has composed music for many Broadway plays, including *Fences*, *Ma Rainey's Black Bottom*, and *Children of a Lesser God*. In 2021, he earned an Emmy nomination for writing the score to *Tulsa Burning*, a History Channel documentary. As a bandleader, he has won three Grammy Awards.

Songs to listen to: "16th St. Baptist Church," "Lazy Mama"

Delfeayo Marsalis, fourth son of Ellis, is a trombonist and Grammy-winning producer. He has recorded eight albums as a leader and has performed with Art Blakey, Max Roach, Ray Charles, and other legendary musicians. He is the founder of the Uptown Jazz Orchestra as well as Uptown Music Theatre, a youth-serving community organization in New Orleans.

Jason Marsalis, Ellis Marsalis's youngest son, is a drummer and vibraphonist. He started playing professional gigs with his father when he was just 7 years old. In his teens, he performed with Lionel Hampton and other greats. His albums as a bandleader include *Heirs of the Crescent City* and *Melody Reimagined: Book 1*.

Geri Allen

Geri Allen was a pianist of remarkable range. On one hand, she could play with experimental artists like Ornette Coleman and Oliver Lake. On the other hand, she could accompany traditional singers like Betty Carter and Mary Wilson of the Supremes. Raised in Detroit, she studied at a high school famous for training world-class jazz musicians. At Howard University, Allen was one of the first students to receive a degree in jazz studies. Later she became an educator herself, teaching first at the University of Michigan and later at the University of Pittsburgh. She recorded more than twenty albums, earning many prizes before her death in 2017. Whether as part of a rhythm section or leading her own group, Allen stood out as a skillful improviser with plenty of imagination.

Roy Hargrove

A trumpeter, composer, and bandleader, Roy Hargrove saw no conflict between jazz and other forms of African American music. He tried to learn from them all, in hopes of creating something new. Born in Texas in 1969, he was discovered by Wynton Marsalis when he was in eleventh grade. Marsalis was so impressed with the young musician that he invited him to sit in during a performance. In 1990, after one year at college, Hargrove went to New York, recording his first album six months after his arrival. In addition to Marsalis, he played with legendary jazz figures like Sonny Rollins and Herbie Hancock. He formed several groups of his own, including a quintet, an eleven-piece Afro-Cuban jazz band called Crisol, a big band, and the RH Factor, which blended jazz, funk, and soul. He worked with many neo-soul and hip-hop artists, including Common, D'Angelo, and Erykah Badu. Hargrove recorded more than twenty albums and won two Grammy Awards before his death in 2018.

Songs to listen to: "Mr. Bruce," "Poetry"

▲ Geri Allen

▲ Bobby McFerrin, Dianne Reeves, Cassandra Wilson

Modern Jazz Singers

Bobby McFerrin's father, Robert McFerrin, was the first Black male singer to solo at the Metropolitan Opera. His mother, Sara Copper, sang in touring Broadway productions and was a longtime music professor. Bobby's success may have been no surprise, then, when his first album came out in 1982. He quickly became known for his lively stage presence, rich voice, and ability to sound like any number of instruments. His fourth album, *Simple Pleasures*, won him a Grammy Award in 1988. Since then, he has performed and recorded with Herbie Hancock, Chick Corea, Yo-Yo Ma, and other musical stars. He has also conducted and written arrangements for orchestras. He has won a total of ten Grammy Awards.

Dianne Reeves recorded her first album in 1981, but it was her 1987 recording that introduced her to a wide audience. A string of stellar albums established her as one of the top jazz vocalists of her era. Born in Chicago in 1956, she was raised in Denver and studied classical voice at the University of Colorado. She has performed or recorded with Clark Terry, Wynton Marsalis, Herbie Hancock, and other top bandleaders. She has also performed with the Chicago Symphony, the Berlin Orchestra, and the Los Angeles Philharmonic. Noted for her clear, strong voice and impressive scat singing, Reeves is a five-time Grammy Award winner.
   Songs to listen to: "Better Days," "Be My Husband"

Her 1993 album, *Blue Light 'Til Dawn*, made a place for **Cassandra Wilson** in any conversation about outstanding vocalists, and not just those who sang jazz. It was the first of several records in which she flavored her jazz with country, blues, folk, rock, and other kinds of music. Born in Jackson, Mississippi, she moved from the South to New York in 1982. She found work with jazz veterans Abbey Lincoln and Henry Threadgill, among others. Nineteen years later, *Time* magazine named her "America's Best Singer." She has won two Grammy Awards.

M-Base

A way of thinking about creating music, M-Base was introduced in the late 1980s by alto saxophonist Steve Coleman and several other artists. In 1991, they released their first album, *Anatomy of a Groove*. Some members involved in M-Base have also had noteworthy solo careers. They include Cassandra Wilson (vocals), Greg Osby (saxophone), Geri Allen (piano), and Robin Eubanks (trombone).

A Tribe Called Quest

The rappers Q-Tip, Phife Dawg, Jarobi White, and DJ Ali Shaheed Muhammad were the members of the Tribe, among the most-acclaimed hip-hop groups ever. In 1991 they released their second album, *The Low End Theory*, offering new connections between rap and jazz. The songs include many passages from bebop and fusion. Art Blakey, Weather Report, and Eric Dolphy are among the artists sampled. In another unusual move, the group hired hard bop legend Ron Carter to come into the studio and record the bass line for one single, "Verses from the Abstract."

The Low End Theory sold more than one million copies and is included on many lists of the best rap albums of all time.

▲ **A Tribe Called Quest**

Don Byron

As a boy in the Bronx, Don Byron took up the clarinet in hopes that it would help with his asthma. Since the 1990s, he has been regarded as one of the best at his instrument. In 1992 he recorded his first album, *Tuskegee Experiments*. His other albums have revisited Motown classics, the compositions of gospel greats Thomas Dorsey and Rosetta Tharpe, and klezmer, a European folk music rooted in Jewish tradition.

Songs to listen to: "Tuskegee Strutter's Ball," "Didn't It Rain"

Joshua Redman

After graduating from Harvard University in 1991, Joshua Redman made plans for law school. Plans changed when he won the Thelonious Monk International Jazz Competition, and chose a career in music instead. The son of respected saxophonist Dewey Redman, Joshua has become a best-selling composer and bandleader. Raised in Berkeley, California, he took up the tenor saxophone at age 10. He played in school bands through high school and college. His first album, *Joshua Redman*, was released in 1993. He has since recorded more than a dozen albums. Along the way, he has performed with Pat Metheny, Chick Corea, Roy Hargrove, and many others.

Guru

With DJ Premier, Guru was one-half of Gang Starr, an acclaimed hip-hop duo. On albums like *No More Mr. Nice Guy* and *Step in the Arena*, the pair had been among the first artists to make hits from a mix of jazz and rap. Other rap groups, including A Tribe Called Quest and Digable Planets, soon followed.

Keith Elam, a Boston native, became interested in a rap career while studying at Morehouse College. He adopted the name Guru, which stands for Gifted Unlimited Rhymes Universal. He founded Gang Starr in 1987. Six years later he launched a solo project, *Jazzmatazz, Vol. 1*. Unlike many similar efforts, the album features live studio performances from a number of notable jazz musicians, including Branford Marsalis, organist Lonnie Liston Smith, and vibraphonist Roy Ayers.

Songs to listen to: "Loungin,'" "Transit Ride"

Christian McBride

Born in Philadelphia in 1972, bassist Christian McBride starting playing professionally at age 17. He worked with Joshua Redman, Milt Jackson, and others before becoming a leader himself. He released his first album, *Gettin' to It*, in 1995. At least a dozen more have followed. His many projects include a trio, a quartet, a quintet, and a seventeen-piece big band. There's also The Christian McBride Situation, in which he plays electric bass. That group explores funk, hip-hop sampling, and turntable techniques like cutting and scratching. In addition, he has been a supporting player on not just jazz records, but R&B, pop, rock, and hip-hop recordings as well. Chick Corea, Pat Metheny, Chaka Khan, James Brown, Sting, and Queen Latifah are just a few of the artists he's worked with. He has recorded more than 300 sessions in total, winning seven Grammy awards along the way.

Songs to listen to: "Fried Pies," "Sand Dune"

▲ **Guru**

Nicholas Payton

Born in 1973, Payton is yet another gifted artist who grew up in the birthplace of jazz. The son of a musician, he began playing trumpet at age 4 and playing in a New Orleans club at age 10.

The arrival in 1995 of his first album, *From This Moment*, announced the emergence of an impressive new talent. Some twenty albums later, he continues to play and record. In addition, he is a dedicated music blogger.

Regina Carter

A Detroit native, Regina Carter started violin lessons at age 4. She didn't discover jazz until age 16. At a concert by the great violinist Stéphane Grappelli, she left dazzled. Determined to make music for a living, she studied at colleges in Boston and Michigan. After graduation it took a while for her to find her way. She released her first album as a leader in 1995 at age 33, but her career didn't begin to take off until 1998. She has recorded ten albums of her own and taken part in studio sessions with Cassandra Wilson, Wynton Marsalis, and others. In recognition of her violin mastery, she was awarded a MacArthur Fellowship in 2006.

Songs to listen to: "Misterioso," "Find Yourself"

◂ **Regina Carter**

Jason Moran

Born in Houston, Texas, in 1975, pianist and composer Jason Moran grew up preferring hip-hop to jazz. When he heard a recording of 'Round Midnight by Thelonious Monk, he changed his mind. After high school, he studied at the Manhattan School of Music. His first professional job was with saxophonist Greg Osby. In 1998 he recorded his first album as band leader. While continuing his own projects, Moran has also performed or recorded with Charles Lloyd, Dave Holland, Christian McBride, and Wayne Shorter, among others. He has composed for stage and multimedia productions. In 2010 he was named a MacArthur Fellow.

Songs to listen to: "Kinda Dukish," "Blue Blocks"

Vijay Iyer

Born in Albany, New York, in 1971, Vijay Iyer began violin lessons at age 3. Today he is celebrated for his skill at playing piano, an instrument for which he's had little formal training. He was studying physics in graduate school when he found a more appealing path. He began a study of how music works while preparing for a career as a pianist. His many recordings and concert performances have brought him much acclaim. He has more than two dozen albums to his credit and composes for other quartets and chamber orchestras. Iyer won a MacArthur Fellowship in 2013. The following year he became the first jazz musician to become a professor at Harvard University.

Songs to listen to: "Human Nature," "Children of Flint"

Billy Childs

In 2006, pianist-composer Billy Childs won three Grammy Awards and attention for an album called Lyric. It was the first in a series of projects that he calls "jazz/chamber music." The music is a blend of classical and jazz traditions, performed by piano, acoustic guitar, harp, woodwinds, bass, and drums.

Childs released his second album, Autumn: In Moving Pictures, in 2010. It earned him two more Grammy Awards. Childs was already an acclaimed performer and composer. His body of work includes several other albums as a leader, six years touring with trumpeter Freddie Hubbard, and performances with Wynton Marsalis. As a composer, he has accepted commissions from the Kronos Quartet, the Lincoln Center Jazz Orchestra, and many others. He has written arrangements for Dianne Reeves, Sting, and Yo-Yo Ma, to name just a few.

Songs to listen to: "Scarborough Fair," "In Carson's Eyes"

▴ **Billy Childs**

The New Generation

With every passing season, some gloomy observers suggest that the glory days of jazz are coming to an end. They say that the appeal of other types of music makes it harder for jazz to get the attention it needs to thrive. But jazz has always had critics who predicted it would just be a passing fad, and each year, its finest artists have proved them wrong. Every generation brings forth new composers, vocalists, and instrumentalists who honor the best traditions of jazz while gazing boldly toward the future. Thanks to their brilliance, jazz remains very much alive, and still very cool.

▲ Kamasi Washington's band

▲ Nicole Mitchell

Nicole Mitchell

Nicole Mitchell is widely regarded as one of the greatest jazz flautists in the United States. She has recorded several albums, and has toured with her band, the Black Earth Ensemble, throughout the U.S. and Europe. She is also admired for the work she does to encourage interest in jazz. Mitchell was the first woman president of the AACM, the musicians' collective we learned about earlier (see page 66). She is also director of the jazz studies program at the University of Pittsburgh.

Songs to listen to: "Soprano Song," "Blessed"

Cécile McLorin Salvant

Cécile McLorin Salvant was born in Miami in 1989. She began piano lessons at age 5 and joined a local choir at 8. She recalls growing up in a house where many types of music were played, including Haitian, hip-hop, soul, classical jazz, gospel, and Cuban music. She was studying law in France when, at 21, she won the Thelonious Monk International Jazz Vocals Competition in Washington, D.C. Before long, she had devoted herself to music full-time. Her concerts and recordings include songs from vaudeville, blues, folk, theater, jazz, and baroque music. A three-time Grammy winner and MacArthur Fellow, she is already one of the most accomplished singers of her generation.

Songs to listen to: "Left Alone," "Thunderclouds"

Esperanza Spalding

▲ Esperanza Spalding

Never in the fifty-three-year history of the Grammy Awards had the Best New Artist prize been given to a jazz artist. That is, not until 2011. Esperanza Spalding, then 26 years old, received the honor over several better-known pop stars. Since that historic night, Spalding, a bassist, has been one of the most recognizable jazz artists on the planet.

She grew up in Portland, Oregon, and showed signs of musical promise when she was very young. Spalding excelled at violin, clarinet, and oboe before discovering her love for the double bass in high school. She recorded her first three albums soon after graduating from Berklee College of Music. She has recorded three more since then, winning three more Grammys along the way. Her compositions reflect her love for many kinds of music, including R&B, Brazilian, and funk. She has exposed jazz to a wider audience by performing with pop stars such as Prince, Janelle Monáe, and Bruno Mars.

Songs to Listen to: "I Know You Know," "Black Gold"

TERRI LYNE CARRINGTON

Terri Lyne Carrington was 7 years old when she inherited her grandfather's drum kit. Long before she was born, he had played with Fats Waller and other jazz legends. By the time she was 11, she had earned a scholarship to Berklee College of Music. By the time she was 23, she had released her first album and played with Herbie Hancock and Wayne Shorter. For many years she has been among the most accomplished jazz drummers in the world.

In 2011 she won her first Grammy Award for *The Mosaic Project*, featuring all women performers. She has won two more, including an award for Best Jazz Instrumental Album in 2014. She is the first female musician to win the honor. A longtime professor at Berklee, she founded the school's Institute of Jazz and Gender Justice in 2018. Her goal is to create more opportunities and recognition for women musicians.

Songs to listen to: "Bells (Ring Loudly)," "Echo"

Robert Glasper

In several of his recorded works, pianist-bandleader Robert Glasper has bridged the gap between jazz and other forms of Black music. *Double Booked*, released in 2010, featured acoustic piano on one side and R&B and hip-hop elements on the other. He won a Grammy Award for *Black Radio* (2012), which included contributions from rappers Yasiin Bey and Lupe Fiasco, as well as vocals from neo-soul singers Lalah Hathaway and Erykah Badu.

Songs to listen to: "Chant," "Smells Like Teen Spirit"

Kamasi Washington

When composer and bandleader Kamasi Washington released his first album in 2015, it excited many jazz fans. Some see the Los Angeles native as the most exciting tenor saxophonist since John Coltrane. His recording *The Epic* won the first-ever American Music Prize, given for the best debut album by an American artist. He has since released a second full-length album, *Heaven and Earth*. He has performed alongside Wayne Shorter, Herbie Hancock, John Legend, Chaka Khan, and various other artists. He composed the score for *Becoming*, a 2020 documentary produced by Michelle Obama.

Songs to listen to: "Clair de Lune," "Sun Kissed Child"

Tyshawn Sorey

Best known as a drummer and composer, Tyshawn Sorey is also a skilled trombonist and pianist. He has performed or recorded with Vijay Iyer, Anthony Braxton, and others. He has composed works for the Louisville Orchestra, the International Contemporary Ensemble, and the Los Angeles Philharmonic, among others. A professor of composition at the University of Pennsylvania, he was awarded a MacArthur Fellowship in 2017.

Songs to listen to: "Untitled Five," "A Cactus and a Rose"

JAZZ AND JUSTICE

Throughout the history of jazz, artists have used their music to call for equality and change. In addition, they have highlighted past injustices or honored heroes and heroines of the struggle for freedom. No decade has passed without performers creating new work to support important causes. Here are just a few examples:

"(What Did I Do to Be So) Black and Blue" by Fats Waller and Andy Razaf

"Strange Fruit" by Billie Holiday

We Insist!: Max Roach's Freedom Now Suite by Max Roach and Abbey Lincoln

"Alabama" by John Coltrane

The Movement Revisited: A Musical Portrait of Four Icons by Christian McBride

Ten Freedom Summers by Wadada Leo Smith

▲ **Max Roach and Abbey Lincoln performing together.**

▲ A scene from the opera *Treemonisha*

Jazz at the Opera

Black composers have been writing operas almost since the dawn of jazz. Scott Joplin's dream project was an opera called *Treemonisha*, written around 1910 and not staged until 1972, long after his death. In the late 1930s, James P. Johnson and the great poet Langston Hughes wrote *De Organizer*, but it was performed only once, at a convention of union members. In 1939, Hughes and William Grant Still tried without success to interest white opera companies in their project, *Troubled Island*. In recent years, more Black jazz composers have succeeded in having their operatic works produced. Here are some of the most prominent examples.

Pianist **Anthony Davis** performs with Episteme, a jazz band he founded in the 1980s. He also has been composing operas for decades. The premiere of his first, *X: The Life and Times of Malcolm X*, took place at the New York City Opera in 1986. He has continued to focus on race and other social issues. A 1997 opera was about the Amistad slave rebellion. His fifth opera, *The Central Park Five*, was about a group of young men falsely charged and imprisoned for a horrible crime. Davis received the Pulitzer Prize for that work in 2020.

In addition to being a first-rate trumpeter, **Terence Blanchard** has excelled at composing for stage and screen. He has written more than forty film scores,

including for *Finding Forrester, Love & Basketball*, and *One Night in Miami . . . .* His second opera, *Fire Shut Up in My Bones*, was presented at the Metropolitan Opera in 2021. It was the first time in the opera house's 138-year history that it staged a production written by an African American composer.

Wayne Shorter and **Esperanza Spalding**, both of whom we met earlier, combined forces in the 2021 debut production of *Iphigenia*, staged in Boston. Shorter, combining his traditional quartet with the kind of orchestra usually found at the opera, wrote the music. Spalding co-wrote the libretto and performed the title role.

JAZZ MUSEUMS AND
PLACES OF INTEREST

American Jazz Museum

1616 E 18th Street
Kansas City, MO 64108

Louis Armstrong House Museum

34-56 107th Street
Queens, NY 11368

**Eubie Blake National Jazz Institute
and Cultural Center**

847 N Howard Street
Baltimore, MD 21201

W.C. Handy House Museum

352 Beale Street
Memphis, TN 38103

Scott Joplin House State Historic Site

2658 Delmar Blvd
St. Louis, MO 63103

The National Jazz Museum

58 W 129th Street
Ground Floor, 2203
New York, NY 10027

New Orleans Jazz Museum

400 Esplanade Ave
New Orleans, LA 70116

Nina Simone Childhood Home

30 E Livingston Street
Tryon, NC 28782

If It Sounds Good . . .

From its roots in African rhythms and the swirling mosaic of Congo Square, jazz has journeyed through the decades, acquiring new shapes and melodies by way of places like Chicago, Kansas City, and New York. Carrying their instruments alongside their mighty imaginations, the geniuses of jazz took their creativity beyond American borders and shared their brilliance across the seas. Thanks to their efforts, jazz remains one of our country's most influential and enduring contributions to world culture. Echoes of this amazing music can now be heard from Berlin to Barcelona, from Mombasa

NEW YORK CITY

BERLIN

BARCELONA

to Mumbai. Throughout its evolution, jazz continues to reflect many different styles and sounds. The artists who keep the music alive haven't always agreed on the best ways to compose and play. But they have seldom differed when it comes to the ultimate purpose of jazz.

What matters in the end is whether or not listening to it brings you joy. As usual, our old friend Duke Ellington probably said it best. "If it sounds good," he said, "it *is* good."

MUMBAI

LONDON

MOMBASA

93

Index

Enjoy the rest of the Child's Introduction series!

A Child's Introduction to African American History

A Child's Introduction to Art

A Child's Introduction to Ballet

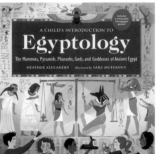

A Child's Introduction to Egyptology

A Child's Introduction to the Environment

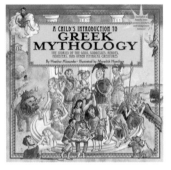

A Child's Introduction to Greek Mythology

A Child's Introduction to Natural History

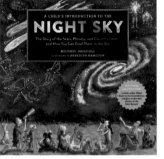

A Child's Introduction to the Night Sky

A Child's Introduction to Norse Mythology

A Child's Introduction to the Nutcracker

A Child's Introduction to the Orchestra

A Child's Introduction to Poetry

A Child's Introduction to Space Exploration

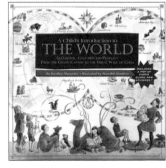

A Child's Introduction to the World